CONTENTS

I0569847

MEDITATION
FOR THE
MODERN MIND

A Beginner's Guide
to Stress Relief and
Emotional Well-Being

B. M. WOLF

INTRODUCTION

In our fast-paced world filled with constant distractions and stressors, the practice of meditation offers a profound refuge for the mind and spirit. Welcome to "Meditation for the Modern Mind: A Beginner's Guide to Stress Relief and Emotional Well-Being." Within these pages, you'll find a treasure trove of timeless wisdom and practical techniques designed to cultivate mindfulness, enhance clarity, and foster a deeper connection with your inner self. Whether you're a novice seeking solace from the chaos of modern life or looking to become a more consistent meditator while deepening your practice, this book serves as a gentle yet powerful companion on your path to well-being.

Drawing from ancient traditions and modern insights, "Meditation for the Modern Mind" demystifies the art of meditation, making it accessible to all who seek its transformative benefits. Through guided exercises, insightful tools, and personal stories of myself and others, you'll embark on a transformative journey to unlock the stillness that lies within. Embrace the present moment, quiet the chatter, and discover the profound joy and peace that arise when you reconnect with the essence of who you are. Get ready to embark on a journey of self-discovery and inner exploration, where each moment becomes an opportunity for profound awakening and deepening awareness.

P.S. We are proud to share that this book is human-written.

CHAPTER ONE
THE MODERN NEED FOR MEDITATION

The alarm goes off, and you hit the ground running. The coffee you are drinking on the way to work spills as you must stop abruptly. We often feel that we're running a day late and a dollar short. Work is stressful. Home is stressful. It seems we cannot get a break from being constantly tugged from one direction to another. We feel that there is no "me-time." There is no time to de-stress and access the emotional well-being that we so crave. In essence, we are working to live... rather than living! The fact is that all these stressors are putting our body and brain into the fight or flight response, which has a lasting effect on us throughout the day. Each one of these responses can last up to an hour before the body goes back to its pre-stress levels. This happens on average eight to fifteen times a day, all at different degrees. What does this mean for you and me? High blood pressure, degradation of digestion, the reproductive system, and growth hormones cease production during fight or flight, along with tissue repair being halted. These are just a few of the things that happen to the body. Outside of the body, we are reactive and defensive; our brain is cluttered and foggy. Our personal and professional relationships suffer from the chronic stress that plagues our modern lifestyle.

UNDERSTANDING STRESS AND ITS IMPACT

THE SCIENCE OF STRESS

Stress is both a physical and psychological reaction to challenges in our lives.[1] It is not a situation in itself which causes stress, but our reaction to it. Since stress is so prevalent in our everyday life, it's important to understand the different forms of stress and how they impact you. There are five main types of stress: good stress, routine stress, acute stress, chronic stress, and traumatic stress.

Good stress, also known as eustress, is seen as beneficial as it supports us in doing our best. Eustress is short-term stress triggered by a specific event, such as playing a game or giving a speech.[2] This small dose of stress helps us to meet deadlines, be productive, show up, and engage in daily life events. **Routine stress** stems from daily pressures that are ongoing and don't stop, such as work, traffic, school, family mealtime, and money problems.[3] **Acute stress** is basically a reaction to an immediate danger or event, such as a flat tire, spilled milk, arguing with a friend, or taking a difficult test. Most people experience routine stress and acute stress daily.[4] **Chronic stress** is ongoing stress related to significant events in our life that seem to have no end, such as relationship problems, career demands, and loss. **Traumatic stress** occurs after the experience of a traumatic event and embeds so deeply in the body that the physiological effects continue to happen even years later.

The underlying biological mechanism of stress is related to the "fight-or-flight" response. "Fight-or-flight" is an evolutionary survival mechanism, enabling humans to save themselves from dangerous situations by either fighting the threat or fleeing. [5] This mechanism was essential for our ancestors to survive life-threatening stressors like being chased by a wild animal. Today, however, the body responds and overreacts to stressors that are not life-threatening, such as losing your phone, arguments, difficulties at work, or being stuck in a traffic jam. To understand the physiological mechanisms underlying the "fight-or-flight" response, it's important to consider how our nervous system functions. The autonomic nervous system has two components: the sympathetic nervous system and the parasympathetic nervous system. The sympathetic nervous system can be seen as a gas pedal. It triggers the "fight-or-flight" response, activating the body to be on high alert so it can deal with the stressor.[5] The parasympathetic nervous system can be seen as a brake. It relaxes the body after the stressor has passed.[5] In the event of a stressful situation, sense organs transmit information about the stressor to the amygdala, a primal area of the brain known for emotional processing. When the amygdala perceives the stressor as dangerous, this part of our brain immediately sends a distress signal to the hypothalamus. The signal activates the sympathetic nervous system via the HPA axis, a network consisting of the hypothalamus, the pituitary gland, and the adrenal glands. Cortisol, a stress hormone, is produced and causes the body to be on high alert to deal with the stressor. When the stressful situation has passed, the parasympathetic nervous system calms the body, and cortisol levels fall again.[5] The problem in our modern world is that most people perceive stressors several times daily, which means the sympathetic nervous system stays activated, and the body is continuously on high alert. After a while, this affects the body and contributes to chronic health problems caused by stress.

COMMON STRESSORS IN MODERN LIFE

Modern life is done with an "on the go" mindset. In our daily lives, there is no space in our schedule to prepare a healthy meal for our lunch break. The time is just enough to grab something processed – we have to hurry, as there is so much traffic. On the way to work, our phone is buzzing with reminders of all the different work projects, and we notice that we have just missed a deadline for an important task. "Of course," you think, "my boss needs everything yesterday!" After a busy day at work, we get home to find ourselves in the usual arguments at the dinner table, and on top of that, there is still the money problem. With this short story, you might have noticed that in just starting our day and getting to work, three out of the five main stress types have already been running: routine, acute, and chronic. And all these stressors keep adding up as we continue our days.

Our physiology keeps stress levels high as there are so many stressors, and the nervous system can't find rest. Instant gratification is at an all-time high. We want everything now as there is no time to wait. Time is money. We rarely take time to connect to our higher self or even permit ourselves to engage in self-care.[6] While there are many stressors in our daily lives, there are also major life events that cause stress. The top life events that cause stress are, in order: the passing of a loved one, divorce, moving, serious illness or injury, and job loss. Currently, I am fifty-one years old and have experienced all of these at least once and several, many times over. Luckily, I am still married to my second husband and have only been severely injured once with a broken foot. We are all in different stages of life, experiencing different life scenarios. Odds are, you have either experienced all these events at least once or will in the future.[7]

THE TOLL ON EMOTIONAL WELL-BEING

As stress continues, it takes a toll on our emotional well-being by making us feel moody, low in energy, irritable, hopeless, anxious, depressed, and guilty for whatever the current circumstance requires. The cognitive impacts of stress include difficulty thinking, memory problems, negative disposition, lack of decision-making skills, and excessive worry.[8] When we look at emotional well-being from a more holistic perspective, we will find that physical and behavioral symptoms of stress also impact our emotional health. Physical signs of stress include headaches, muscle tightness, stomach problems, loss of sex drive, rapid heart rate, high blood pressure, and fatigue. If stress impacts your behavior, symptoms include changes in eating or sleeping patterns, becoming socially withdrawn, nervous habits like nail biting, increased use of caffeine, cigarettes, alcohol, or other drugs, neglect of family or work responsibilities, and decline in performance or productivity.[8]

Stress skews our perspective as our brain is trying to figure out if we should fight or flee, and once a decision is made, the next stressor already presents itself. It's an ongoing circle of being caught in the "fight-or-flight" response.

High levels of stress take a toll on everything from relationships with our families to being able to gain positive traction toward a promotion at work. In essence, being confronted with so many stressors daily makes us feel overwhelmed and unable to get away from stress. We become concerned about the impact of stress on our health and our relationships. We have the intention to engage in self-care practices and to start a meditation routine, but we either can't find the time to even get started, or we try a few times without success. We become frustrated and react to situations in a defensive way. And yet, we would love to experience more calmness and joy and bring these qualities into the world, but we don't know how.

This all sounds quite dramatic, but unfortunately, it's the reality of our modern life. And yet, there are ways to experience daily life without being in a constant state of stress. This is where meditation comes in. Practicing meditation allows us to find our zen zone – a mental state of complete focus and tranquility. Meditation can transform our entire lives as it considers all aspects of an individual, including the body, mind, and spirit. Throughout the book, you will be guided through simple mindfulness tools, receive answers to all your questions, and you will feel better prepared for a consistent meditation practice. As you will see, the impact of meditation on stress is wonderful. You will find yourself asking, "Why is this not taught in school?"

As we continue our deep dive into meditation, you will learn the benefits of what ancient wisdom can do for our modern life. You will see what significant impact a consistent practice will have on your life and those around you. You will learn practical tools for maintaining your own personal zen zone within. This will lead you to more clarity, better decision-making skills, the ability to not open your mouth and insert your foot, speak with more grace, and show up with more compassion and courage.

THE POWER OF MEDITATION

HISTORICAL ROOTS AND MODERN RELEVANCE

Meditation is thousands of years old and has roots in religion, but it's not exclusively a religious practice. Ancient Vedic texts are considered some of the oldest texts on meditation and were passed down orally from the 15th century BCE to the 5th century BCE. Four books make up the texts known as the Vedas. These are some of the earliest teachings on meditation, originating from the Hindu tradition.[9] Around 588 BCE, Buddha, after living as an ascetic and practicing Hinduism for six years, meditated under the Bodhi Tree with a total resolution for 49 days and became enlightened. Buddha simply means "the enlightened one," and Bodhi translates to enlightenment. Buddhism started in India with the birth of Buddha (563 BCE to 483 BCE) but has largely been adopted by Asian countries.[10] Many forms of Buddhism encourage an ascetic lifestyle, renouncing material desires and prejudices in pursuit of spiritual liberation. Often, Buddhists show detachment from material life. The path of Buddhism offers teachings based on compassion and non-violence. It is focused on meditation to get a deeper understanding of the nature of reality and to achieve spiritual enlightenment.

Since ancient times, many forms of meditation have emerged. The famous quote "as many monks, as many paths" refers to the fact that there is a meditation path for everyone. In the classical system of Yoga, meditation is achieved through *Pranayama*, the regulation of the breath; *Pratyahara*, the withdrawal of senses from their objects; and *Dharana*, concentration. These practices lead to meditation, known as *Dhyana,* which progresses further to absorption in the essence of reality, or ecstasy, known as *Samadhi.* An interesting form of meditation is *Japa*, which focuses on the repetition of a mantra or Divine name. Meditation is also known in religions such as Christianity. The bible mentions meditate or meditation 23 times, with 19 of them being found in the Book of Psalms.[11] There are many worldly practices, other than the ones mentioned, that include meditation as a

7

fundamental practice of their philosophy or faith. Meditation does not hold favor to any culture or religion, as the practice of mindfulness can be partnered with any belief system. Think of meditation as your daily mental exercise rather than a religious practice.[12]

BENEFITS OF MEDITATION FOR STRESS REDUCTION

Stress and negative emotions come from a place of fear. Today, we are not thinking, "The copy machine just broke; I'm sure it will be taken care of soon." Instead, we get irritated and annoyed; we feel scared because we have to print an important document at the last minute before a meeting, and we might snap at our co-workers or have an icy disposition. The brain perceives this as a threat and releases the "fight-or-flight" response hormones. 80% of the communication our brain receives travels up through the vagus nerve, which is the main nerve of our parasympathetic nervous system. This is also the passage of the stress response to the brain. When the copy machine breaks, the response happens as if we were being chased by a bear or a tiger. Once upon a time, this served us very well, as it helped us to survive life-threatening situations. In modern times, we most often do not need it. However, for our brain, it looks like we are chased by a wild animal several times a day. And it goes even further - according to the American Psychological Association, in our modern world, the six leading causes of death linked to stress are heart disease, cancer, lung ailments, accidents, cirrhosis of the liver, and suicide. In ancient times, the leading cause of death was infection. Although we have come a long way with modern medicine, and infection is no longer a leading cause of death, it is now stress.

Meditation helps our bodies to relax and restore much-needed calmness by stopping our adrenal glands from producing so much cortisol. It has profound effects on everything from lowering blood pressure and improving heart rate variability to enhancing immune function. Meditation is also known to slow down the aging process of our mind, which reduces signs of aesthetic aging. Practicing meditation also helps to develop a peaceful mind with more clarity and creativity and can make it easier to quit smoking, drinking, and drugs. Research found that meditation can even alter the brain. A study by Dr. Sara Lazar shows that those who participated in an 8-week mindfulness meditation program showed changes in the hippocampus and the amygdala, which are brain areas related to memory, sense of self, empathy, and stress.[13] Another study found that participation in a virtual meditation program led to a reduction in perceived stress, improved sleep quality, and promoted empathy, acceptance, and inner peace.[14] The benefits of meditation have been known for thousands of years, and now, finally, we have science to back them up. This has only happened in the past 30 years or so, and it's expected that the research interest in meditation will only grow in the coming years. At this point, thousands of studies have been conducted on the benefits of meditation, and the few benefits listed here are just a handful of a longer list of benefits.

People who meditate regularly often report reduced stress, better sleep, enhanced emotional well-being, improved concentration, and more harmonious relationships. For instance, a corporate executive might find that daily meditation helps them stay calm and focused in high-pressure situations, ultimately leading to better decision-making and improved job performance. People struggling with insomnia or disrupted sleep patterns have found relief through meditation. By practicing mindfulness or other meditation techniques, they learn to relax and quiet their minds, making it easier to drift off to sleep and to stay asleep. Meditation can also be a powerful tool for managing emotions. Individuals dealing with depression, anger, or grief may find that meditation helps them process their feelings and develop a more positive outlook on life. Students and professionals often use meditation to enhance their ability to concentrate and study. They may find that meditation helps them stay more focused, leading to better academic or work-related outcomes. Improved communication, empathy, and patience are benefits of meditation that can positively impact personal relationships. Couples and families often find that meditation helps them relate to each other more harmoniously.

As we start our meditation practice, at first, we meditate for ourselves, but as we continue with our practice, we realize that we meditate for everyone else too. The small, subtle shifts that happen with consistent practice show up as we engage with our families, friends, and the world as a whole. We often think that meditation practice ends when we get up from our cushion, but the real practice starts as we step back into the world. All the benefits we cultivate with our practice are shared with the world as we become more loving, compassionate, and less reactive, both towards ourselves and others. The results of meditation can vary from person to person; it is not an exact science... but it's a practice for everyone, worthy of exploration.

REAL-LIFE SUCCESS STORIES

A student of mine, let's call her Anna, used to suffer from stress, depression, and social anxiety for many years. She tried to meditate occasionally, but she couldn't see any changes in her life. She explained to me that she couldn't meditate and that she didn't enjoy the practice. When we looked at the form of meditation she practiced, we found that it was a rather strict form of meditation inspired by Buddhism, which encourages practitioners to sit still in one position, not to move, and to become aware of all thoughts. Anna reported that as soon as she sat down to meditate and closed her eyes, it felt like there were thousands of thoughts going through her mind, and she didn't know how to stop thinking. I explained to her that meditation, in the beginning, is not about ceasing all thought activity but about exploring our inner world, cultivating love and peace, and, from there, finding gaps in our thoughts. Anna was surprised, and her guilt for having so many thoughts and seemingly not being able to meditate ceased. She tried another, more heart-based form of meditation that focuses on connecting back to love in our hearts. After meditating like this for just a few days, she reported to me that she now enjoys her meditation practice and looks forward to this part of her day. After a few weeks, she noticed significant changes in her life, as she seemed much happier, less stressed, and more relaxed in social situations.

This story highlights the importance of finding a form of meditation we love and emphasizing enjoyment overstrain.

SETTING THE STAGE FOR YOUR MEDITATION JOURNEY

CREATING A SUPPORTIVE ENVIRONMENT

Starting a meditation practice is much easier than you might think. You can do it from the comfort of your home, and no special clothing or equipment is required. The first important step is to create your meditation place. This is called a *Zen Den* or *Peace Pod*, which is a space solely dedicated to your practice. Ideally, this space looks beautiful to you, and you enjoy coming back for your meditation practice. The invitation is to make your space sacred, as it should be a reminder of your intention to practice stillness and to go within.[15] To create your *Zen Den*, find somewhere comfortable in your home to sit or lie down. For myself, I use a Papasan chair with a pillow and blanket, and I can shut the door so as not to be disturbed. I have some of my favorite crystals, a candle and journal, incense, and headphones all there to support me in my practice. You can add any items that inspire you, such as a singing bowl, pillows, pictures, or mala beads, which is a necklace with 108 beads. You may want to include spiritual or religious texts if that is what is important to you. There are also beautiful poetry books, and some people enjoy it to start their meditation practice with an inspiring quote.

Some philosophies state you need to be in a certain position, in a certain manner, at a certain time early in the morning. If you are a person who thrives with more structure, this could be the way for you. It is important to find a way that works well for you. As my teacher, davidji would say, "Comfort is Queen." There is no wrong or right way to start. Just begin. If you are not comfortable, you will most likely not come back to your practice. Make it comfortable and enjoyable for you. It's also advisable to let other people in the house know what you are doing so they don't disturb you. Ideally, your meditation environment is quiet and private, and you can close the door.

OVERCOMING COMMON OBSTACLES

There are some meditation myths out there that prevent many people from even beginning a practice. People often share with me, "I can't meditate because my mind will not be quiet." The truth is that at the beginning, the only time your mind will be quiet is if you are in a coma or dead. None of us want that. Your brain will chatter just as your heart will beat. The goal is to disconnect from the chatter, much like a cloud passing by in the sky. We are like the clear, blue sky, the awareness on which the thoughts or clouds appear. We are looking for the space in between our chatter. It is the nature of thoughts to come, stay a bit, and pass, just like clouds. We can make a choice to stay focused on the clouds, or we can focus on the clear blue sky beyond them.

Another obstacle is expectation. Expecting something to happen during meditation that is transcendent or special is another misnomer about meditation. Nothing is supposed to happen. If it does, great; if not, that's okay too! Meditation is a brief departure from the chaos of life that instills calm and brings us back to equilibrium. Therefore, an important attitude for meditation is equanimity. If you constantly find yourself wanting to experience something special during meditation, this is just another thought to be observed.

Often, I hear a student saying, "I'm not doing it right!" There is no right or wrong way to do this. The best way is whatever way feels good for you and inspires you to continue meditation. Since there are so many forms of meditation, there is a lot to explore, and there is a meditation path for you.

A common obstacle to meditation is the perception that we do not have time – but, as we all know, we make time for what is important to us. It can help you integrate meditation into your daily routine and find a time during which you meditate every day. It is good to not expect any significant changes in your life after your first meditation. Just like anything, the benefits of meditation are felt with consistent practice. Quietly and subtly, they will sneak into your life until you stop and look back on your life before meditation.

THE COMMITMENT TO CHANGE

All it takes to start a meditation practice is commitment and willingness to integrate your practice into your daily routine. To begin your meditation practice, commit to yourself and set your morning alarm 10 minutes earlier first. You don't need to jump headfirst for 30 minutes a day or longer. "When eating an elephant, take small bites." Start small, and gradually add a minute a week until you are at your desired time commitment.

It's also beautiful to set an intention for starting your meditation practice and to know your "why." Perhaps, while reading this chapter and becoming more aware of how stress impacts your life, you found some reasons that inspire you to practice meditation. You can write them into your journal to foster a commitment to yourself and your practice, and you can refer to these reasons whenever you lose motivation. Your "why" can be like a guiding light during your meditation journey and guide you throughout this book.

CHAPTER TWO
HOW TO START MEDITATING IN A WORLD THAT DOESN'T SEEM TO STOP

"What if meditation isn't about emptying your mind, but rather embracing the fullness of your inner world? What lies beneath the surface when you close your eyes and meditate?"

THE FOUNDATIONS OF MEDITATION

POSTURE AND COMFORT

The poet Rumi said: *"Close your eyes, fall in love, stay here."* In our modern world, meditation is often understood to be about emptying our minds and ceasing all thought activity. While calming the mind is indeed an essential part of meditation, in essence, this practice is about getting to know ourselves in depth. Meditation invites us to explore our inner world, look beneath the surface, and discover who we really are. And inevitably, this will lead us to fall in love with ourselves again.

Most importantly, meditation is accessible to everyone. We all know the story of the Buddha and ancient meditation masters, who sat still in a complicated meditation position for days or weeks until they reached enlightenment. As our practice deepens, a strong meditation posture and dedication to our practice becomes significant. In the beginning, however, we can meditate in any comfortable position, and with this, meditation is easily accessible. In fact, for beginners, the most important feature of a meditation posture is comfort. I can testify to the importance of this by sharing the experience of one of my students. When she had just started meditating many years ago, she went to a 10-day silent meditation retreat. Starting on day four, students were advised to sit completely still, without moving, for three hours a day. This might be helpful for an advanced meditator; for my student, however, as a beginner, it seemed impossible. She explained that rather than relaxing and lovingly observing herself, she got frustrated as she had to change her posture every 15 minutes. And, of course, everyone around her seemed to sit entirely still for an hour! Luckily, though, this was the beginning of her meditation journey, not the end.

As a rule for beginners, we can say that the meditation posture should be a comfortable sitting posture with a straight spine. However, if you are uncomfortable, you will not return to your practice. If you have back pain, grab a pillow for support. If you need to lie down, lie down. As I shared earlier, my comfortable spot is a papason chair with a pillow for back support... with legs in a comfortable lotus position. My dog, Lola, snuggles up with me for meditation every morning. If you want to start with a stronger posture, try sitting cross-legged on a cushion or in a chair with your back straight and your feet on the floor. The eyes can be gently closed, or you can find a still gazing point. For this, it is best to pick something natural and not too complicated, like a flame, a leaf, a twig, or a flower.[1] If you are an advanced meditator and would like a challenge, you can also try the posture of the Buddha Vairocana.[2] For this, you sit on the floor in a lotus or half-lotus position, the left leg over the right leg. The hands are placed in the cosmic mudra, with the palms facing upwards and the right hand placed on

15

the left hand. The spine is straight, with the neck aligned and the chest gently open. The tongue is touching the palate behind the upper teeth gently, and the eyes are open with the gaze placed one or two meters in front.

BREATHING TECHNIQUES

Breathing and breath techniques are a fundamental part of meditation. In traditional scriptures, controlled breathing techniques are known as *pranayama*. They are related to the flow of *prana*, or life force, in the body. *Pranayama* can help to quiet the mind and alter our emotional states, and it has numerous benefits for the physical body. For instance, breathing techniques can easily and effortlessly slow down your heart rate variability and lower your blood pressure.[3] The benefits of controlled breathing also include expanding the surface space of your lungs with the inhale, which means more oxygen receptors are activated. When we hold our breath, we are giving more time for the exchange of oxygen and CO^2. In general, if we perceive stress, there is a build-up of CO^2 in our blood as we often take shallow breaths, which leads to agitation and unclear thinking. When we return to slow, deep breathing, the CO^2 in our blood is balanced.[4]

A basic but important breathing technique is the full yogic breath. In daily life, we tend to take shallow breaths into the chest, but the healthiest way to breathe is to inhale into the abdomen. To take deep, full breaths, you can place one hand on your chest and one on your belly. Take a long, deep breath in through your nose, fill your lungs completely, and let the air move further down to expand your abdomen until the hand on your belly rises. Exhale through your nose and observe the abdomen returning to its original position. Repeat these steps as often as you like and open yourself to deep peace and relaxation.

Another breathing technique for beginners is box breathing, which is a deep breathing technique known as *sama vritti pranayama*. It helps calm the nervous system, decrease stress in the body, and embrace inner peace. It's a powerful technique that can be applied many times during the day. This breathing technique is called box breathing because we breathe in squares to a count of four.[5] You breathe in for the count of 4, hold for the count of 4, exhale for the count of 4, and hold for the count of 4. For box breathing, make sure to sit comfortably, gently close your eyes if you feel like it, and breathe in and out through the nose while slowly counting to four.

Try beginning and finishing meditation with deep breathing. Also, breath techniques can be practiced at any point during the day. They're great for small breaks at work, or anytime you feel stressed, to help bring your body back to a calmer state and to focus the mind on the present moment.

MINDFULNESS VS. CONCENTRATION

An important distinction can be made between mindfulness, meditation, and concentration.

Mindfulness is the ability to be fully present in the moment and deeply engaged with what we are doing while being at peace with the present moment as it is.[6] When walking in nature and you are aware of the natural world around you without being lost in thoughts, you are engaged in mindfulness practice.

Concentration, or *dharana*, is the action of focusing one's attention on a particular object, such as the breath. The concentration prepares the mind for meditation, as we can only access deeper states of consciousness when the mind is quiet and able to focus one-pointedly on a particular object. When you are in nature and decide to focus all your attention on a beautiful flower, you are engaged in concentration.

Meditation is about drifting deeply within, beyond any activity of the mind. Meditation is what happens in the gaps between thoughts, in the space between all the chatter. Meditators often say, "I'll see you in the gap." When you drift deeper into an inner stillness, a spaciousness that is beyond thoughts, you are practicing meditation.

MINDFULNESS MEDITATION

CULTIVATING AWARENESS

Cultivating awareness is living in the present moment instead of acting on compulsions. Meditation practice and sitting in silence are essential ways to develop awareness. Outside of formal practice, we can bring awareness to every aspect of our day-to-day lives. This is our real practice: As we go through our days, observing the chatter and making conscious choices.[7] Usually, we function on autopilot – we wake up, dress, have a quick breakfast, and rush to work. As we start bringing awareness to all these aspects of our daily lives, our quality of life increases as we live in the joy of the present moment. We become less triggered and reactive, and we start enjoying whatever we are doing. Yes, even traffic jams can be a wonderful practice to cultivate awareness. Rather than reacting to the frustration you feel, and the anxiety as you are already late for work, observe yourself and get curious as to why you are reacting in a certain way in this situation. Asking yourself, "Why did I react that way?" is an important starting point for cultivating awareness.

Let's dive a bit deeper into what awareness truly means. In some traditions, this awareness is referred to as Witness Consciousness. It is that inner, silent awareness that always exists, even in the absence of thoughts. In many traditions, the need to cultivate self-awareness is described as the most crucial element of cultivating a meditation practice. In classical Indian texts on meditation, the nature of reality is described as *"Sat-chit-ananda"* – pure existence, pure awareness, and pure bliss. Through cultivating a meditation practice, *sat-chit-ananda* will be revealed as our true essence. Usually, we are not aware of this background of pure existence, awareness, and bliss as we are constantly lost in thoughts and mental chatter. As we learn to observe them and cultivate awareness, the witness consciousness will shine through us.

A beautiful meditation exercise to cultivate awareness is visualizing our thoughts as clouds. Start in a comfortable seated position and close your eyes if you feel like it. Then, be open to whatever thoughts are arising. Once you become aware of a thought, visualize it as a cloud passing in front of you. As more thoughts arise, visualize them all as clouds. Some might be dark, others lighter, some big, and some small. They might cover the entire sky. Once you feel complete, take a few moments to observe all the thoughts as clouds. Let them come, stay a bit, and pass. You will notice that this creates spaciousness – you used to be identified with all these thoughts, and now you just witness them. Shift your awareness from the clouds back to the clear blue sky beneath the clouds. You are this clear blue sky; you are the awareness on which all these thoughts appear. For a few moments, rest in this pure awareness. Once you are ready, you can conclude the exercise and open your eyes.

Another meditation to cultivate awareness is to rest in the pure "I AM." In traditional texts, the I-feeling is referred to as *"Aham Vritti."* It is this pure feeling of existence before any labels, thoughts, or emotions. In our meditation, we can focus all our attention on this pure "I AM"-feeling, which will take us deeper into awareness. Even as thoughts are occurring, as soon as we are aware, we come back to the "I AM." We can extend this exercise beyond our meditation practice and stay anchored in the "I AM" as we go through our day. This beautiful quote by Nisargadatta Maharaj illustrates the process: *"Go back to the state of pure being, where the 'I AM' is still in its purity before it got contaminated with 'this I am' or 'that I am.' Your burden is of false self-identification – abandon them all. I simply followed my Guru's instruction which was to focus my mind on pure being "I AM" and stay in it. I used to sit for hours together with nothing but the 'I AM' in my mind, and soon peace and joy and a deep, all-embracing love became my normal state."*

DEALING WITH DISTRACTIONS

When starting a meditation practice, the mind will automatically travel to thoughts, sounds, and physical sensations. This is not a time to self-criticize or to think, "See, I can't do this." It's ok, a normal occurrence. It's the nature of the mind to wander and be distracted. Easily and effortlessly, come back to the breath, the mantra, the mala beads, or whatever tool you are using for meditation. In the beginning, it's beneficial to choose a tool before starting a meditation session. This tool will then act as an anchor to bring you back to awareness when a thought distracts you. In the beginning, the recommended tool would be your breath. You can become aware of your natural breath as it flows in and out of your nostrils. Whenever you get distracted, you gently return your focus to the breath. Other tools you can add over time are reciting a specific mantra or mala beads. When you feel your mind going down the rabbit hole, making lists, living in the past or the future, as soon as you realize, just come back to your tool. If you have to start over every 60 seconds, it's ok. As Lisa Kohn said: "Every breath is a chance to begin again."

Whatever the distraction may be, it can help us to cultivate awareness. In this sense, rather than judging the distraction, we make it serve us. Let's say you sit in meditation, and a thought keeps occurring about a problematic relationship in your life. Your attention goes back and forth between resting in awareness and thoughts about the problem. You are in the phase of developing concentration, *dharana*. Every time the thought occurs, you use it as a reminder to come back to concentrate on your anchor. Over time, you will see that while at the beginning you spent several minutes getting lost in the story about the relationship, after a while of practicing, after just a few seconds of the thought appearing again, you see the thought and shift back to awareness. Eventually, this will lead you into a meditative state of resting in pure awareness, *dhyana*. Being able to use the relationship problem to come back to awareness will have a positive impact on your daily life. As you feel less stressed by the relationship problem, you perceive it with more spaciousness and don't react immediately. And this process works in the same way for any recurring thoughts!

MEDITATION APPS AND RESOURCES

There are some great meditation apps and resources available to help us start our meditation journey. One of the most popular meditation apps is Insight Timer [8], with a library of over 100k free meditations on many different subjects. There are also live sessions, talks, meditation music, and a meditation timer. The app offers a lot of valuable content for free, or you can get a subscription to access meditation courses.

Another popular app is Headspace [9] It offers many meditations to manage feelings and thoughts. The focus is on developing mindfulness for everyday mental health.

Calm [10] is another well-known meditation app that focuses on meditation to manage stress, anxiety, and sleep problems and to cultivate more presence in everyday life. The main emphasis is on calming the mind.

It's a great idea to try different apps to see which one you resonate with. My personal favorite is Insight Timer. Sometimes, I just need a little natural sound for meditation, like ocean waves or a crackling fire, and sometimes the sounds of koshi chimes. Insight Timer has everything from fully guided meditations to simple timers with soft ending sounds that are customizable. The app measures how many minutes you spend meditating and gives stars for milestones reached. You can even connect with other meditators in your geographical area. Thousands of people are meditating on the app at any given time, which is fun to see. Another benefit of Insight Timer is that it supports your personal meditation journey. You can start with guided meditations on different topics and then start using the timer for your meditations.

GUIDED MEDITATION AND VISUALIZATION

THE ROLE OF GUIDED SESSIONS

According to my insightful teacher, davidji, all meditations are guided. You are either guiding yourself or letting someone else guide you. I have no reason to disagree. He has deep wisdom on meditation, which he shares with millions of people worldwide and teaches people the power of meditation to heal their hearts and create their dream lives.[11] *"When the student is ready the teacher will appear. When the student is truly ready... The teacher will disappear." Tao Te Ching.*

21

Guided meditations come in many forms, from body scans and imagining yourself sitting by the ocean to listening to a teacher like davidji guide you down a path or into mantra repetition. If you are new to meditation, listening to meditations guided by someone else is the easiest way to start. Even for advanced practitioners, sometimes it's nice just to let go and surrender into the calm space someone else's voice is providing.

Three common forms of guided meditation are mindfulness, stress reduction, and relaxation.[12] During guided mindfulness meditation, we train the mind to stay calm. We let the chatter of the mind continue as it always does, but instead of becoming lost in it, we focus the mind on the present moment by using our anchor. Guided stress reduction meditation introduces techniques to remain more relaxed when stressors are present. Often, they are offered as courses, such as the Mindfulness-Based Stress Reduction (MBSR) program. Guided relaxation meditations are soothing meditations focused on letting go of tensions. Often, calming sounds and peaceful environments are used to help people find deep relaxation and sleep.

VISUALIZATION TECHNIQUES

Visualization is a form of meditation where we visualize an image or concept and keep our attention focused on it for the duration of the practice. Visualization can be powerful as we use the mind and engage it to create mental images.[13] Visualization can guide us to see ourselves and the world differently, as it uses the unlimited creative potential of our minds. Many people successfully use visualization to change their thoughts, feelings, and behaviors and, with this, to create a new life for themselves. Visualization has become an important tool for transformation and achieving our highest potential.

Visualization can be categorized into two primary forms: Firstly, techniques that focus on visualizing a tangible object outside the body, for example, the sun or the sky. Secondly, some methods focus on actively creating an image from within, such as visualizing your higher self. Examples of visualizations focusing on outside objects are yantra meditations, focused on geometric patterns, and deity meditations by evoking a spiritual teacher or certain gods and goddesses. Any other object that has meaning for you can also be used, such as a beautiful flower, a candle flame, the face of a loved one, or your favorite place. Examples of visualizations focused on creating an inside image are chakra meditation, which focuses on the different energy centers in the body, color breathing, and loving-kindness meditation, in which you imagine yourself sending love and kindness to other beings. We will explore many of these visualization meditations in more detail later in this book.

INNER JOURNEYS TO CALMNESS

Choosing to embark on inner journeys back to calmness is always a choice. Yes, you heard me, it is a choice. We can choose to live in this moment, or we can choose to let our brain dissect every moment, breath, scenario, and any single thing it can get its egoic dendrite on. We want to grow different neural pathways, gain a new perspective, and let go of being right. Who's really right anyway?

We are all the same in that we are looking for inner calmness and peace. Many of us even speak about achieving world peace. And so, we do our daily meditation practice, book the next weekend retreat, or go off into the mountains for a week. Afterwards, we feel so calm. But what happens once we step back into our modern, busy world? Often, we find ourselves reacting to the same stressors, displaying the same tendencies, and losing that sense of calmness rather quickly. Why is that? In a beautiful metaphor, humans are compared to a lake.[14] At their core, every human is calm, beautiful, and peaceful, like a clear lake. But just as the wind disrupts the surface of the still lake and causes waves, the external world shakes up the calmness and peace we all have inside of us. Then, when faced with the stressors of the modern world, it is up to us: We can remember that peace is always within us, no matter what happens, or we forget our true nature and our calmness.

As we meditate, sit in silence, or go on vacation without the stressors of the world, we remember the silence of our true being and the deep peace that comes with it. Then, we interact with the world, and the peace seems gone. As we go through our days, the chatter of the mind is so loud we get lost in stories and labeling the world. In short, we are the commentators of our lives rather than the participants. [15] To stay connected to the peace within, we must remember to be the participant again, which means we simply exist. We find back to the present moment, the natural flow of life. As Eckhart Tolle says: *"As soon as you honor the present moment, all unhappiness and struggle dissolve, and life begins to flow with joy and ease. When you act out the present-moment awareness, whatever you do becomes imbued with a sense of quality, care, and love - even the most simple action."*

Something I often share with meditation students is that the only thing we have any control over in life whatsoever is how we engage with others, how we show up, and how we react. That's it. Everything else is out of our control. The more we embrace this, the quicker we will find the calm, making itself known in our lives.

When I first started meditating in my teenage years, I did body scans to help me fall asleep. My mind would chatter at a fearful and alarming pace. It was in the 80's, and there were no meditation books on my shelf or internet to help me. It happened naturally and set me on a lifelong path. Looking back, these body scans enabled me to bring myself into the present moment, relax enough to calm the chatter, and ever so gently fall asleep. Body scans bring a sense of calm and are similar to getting a massage but for your energy rather than the physical tissue.[16] I would play with a ball of white light or cascading white light and sometimes visualize it as water. It was pure magic for me. I am unsure who the first person ever to say this was; it certainly was not me: "Where attention goes, energy flows."

CHAPTER THREE
STRESS REDUCTION: MEDITATION TECHNIQUES

55% of Americans are stressed out, which, according to stress.org [1], is 20% higher than the international level. 52% of Gen Z have been diagnosed with mental health issues, and women tend to be more stressed than men overall. Get this: 63% of US workers are ready to quit their jobs because of stress. What if all this meditation mumbo jumbo really worked? What if it helped us to all become less reactive and handle unexpected or expected stressful situations with more grace and courage? Let's dive in!

MINDFUL BREATHING FOR IMMEDIATE RELIEF

THE POWER OF BREATH AWARENESS

Often, when we are stressed, we take shallow breaths or even hold our breath. As mentioned previously, this allows CO^2 to build up in our bloodstream, clogging our ability to think clearly and causing agitation and confusion. Often, movies will reference the impact of stress on our breath by showing someone nearly hyperventilating to take a deep breath. Considering that most US workers are experiencing high levels of stress, this unhealthy way of breathing is not just an isolated phenomenon but a problem for much of the population and probably for most people in this modern world. Since many of us are in a constant state of stress, we are consistently breathing in a shallow way, and we must, therefore, bring awareness to our breath.

Breathwork, among other techniques, is a powerful pattern interrupt. When we take a long, slow, deep breath in with a long, slow, deep breath out, this sends a signal to the brain telling us that we are safe and there is no need for the fight or flight response to go off. You might recall the deep breathing technique from the previous chapter, in which you breathe deeply into your abdomen. You can start incorporating this technique in your everyday life until it stops being a technique and starts becoming your new natural way of breathing. Deep, slow breathing is an instant way to de-escalate our reactivity and reduce our levels of perceived stress. In the following, we will look at some more breathing techniques that you can apply in everyday life.

BOX BREATHING, BREATH COUNTING, AND NADI SHODHANA

A well-known breathing technique for beginners is box breathing, which is a deep breathing technique known as *sama vritti pranayama*. It helps calm the nervous system, decrease stress in the body, and embrace inner peace. It's a powerful technique that can be applied many times during the day. This breathing technique is called box breathing because we breathe in squares to a count of four.[2] You breathe in for the count of 4, hold for the count of 4, exhale for the count of 4, and hold for the count of 4. For box breathing, make sure to sit comfortably, gently close your eyes if you feel like it, and breathe in and out through the nose while slowly counting to four.

Once you feel comfortable breathing at a count of 4, you can increase the count to 6, 8, or 10. For example, you breathe in on a count of 6, hold the breath on a count of 6, breathe out to a count of 6, and again hold the breath on a count of 6. Never go above a count of 10, and make sure that the four phases of the breathing cycle remain equal. You can practice 10-20 rounds, and you can gradually increase the duration of the practice to 30-45 minutes.

Alternatively, you can do a short five or ten-minute practice whenever you feel stressed in your day-to-day life.

Another excellent breathing technique for beginners is 6 – 4 – 8. Inhale to the count of 6, hold for the count of 4, and release to the count of 8. For a little extra step, at the top of the breath as you reach 6, take one more inhale to top it off, then hold for the count of 4 and release for the count of 8.

A breathing technique for those who are a bit more advanced is called Nadi Shodhana, also called alternate nostril breathing.[3] It is a powerful technique to relax the nervous system, develop a calm and clear mind, and balance your emotions. *Nadi* is a Sanskrit word for "channel," and *shodhana* translates to "purification." This means that alternate nostril breathing purifies the *nadis* or subtle energy channels of the body.[4] To prepare for the practice Nadi Shodhana, assume a comfortable seating position with your spine straight and your eyes gently closed. The left hand is placed in *chin mudra*, on your left knee, with the index finger and thumb touching and the rest of the fingers stretched. The right hand is placed in *nasagra mudra*, for which you place your index finger and middle finger on your forehead, in between the eyebrows. Your ring finger and little finger are placed on the left nostril, and the thumb on the right nostril. To start the practice, follow the steps:[5]

1. Breathe in deeply, and when you breathe out, close your right nostril with the thumb and exhale through your left nostril.
2. Inhale through your left nostril, then close the left nostril with your ring finger. Release the thumb from the right nostril and breathe out through the right nostril.
3. Inhale through the right nostril. Again, close the right nostril with your thumb and exhale through the left nostril. Inhale through the left nostril.
4. Continue this way and practice for around five minutes. Make sure you keep taking slow, long breaths. Ensure that you are comfortable at all times.

(Photo Credit: Stock Photo in Canva)

5. Conclude your practice by breathing out through the left nostril.

USING BREATH AWARENESS DURING A STRESSFUL SITUATION

One of my students, let's call him Jonathan, used to feel extremely stressed whenever he entered his workplace. No matter what he did, he showed physical and emotional symptoms of stress: nervousness, shallow breathing, anxiety, and racing thoughts about the day ahead. Not surprisingly, this affected his work performance, and he never was able to build deeper connections with his co-workers. After he started to meditate at home for a few weeks, he felt ready to begin his workday with meditation. He arrived at his office fifteen minutes earlier and started to practice box breathing. He would also return to this practice anytime during the day when he noticed a lot of stress in his body. It didn't take long until Jonathan noticed a remarkable difference; his stress levels went down. He could relax into his body again and felt much more clarity and joy about his work. His colleagues and manager noticed the changes in him, as Jonathan could now show his potential and slowly connect more with his co-workers. Eventually, he got a promotion, which he secretly wanted for many years! This is the power of consistent breath awareness practice in situations in life that feel stressful and perhaps have been pressing us for a while.

BODY SCAN MEDITATION

BODY SCAN MEDITATION

As mentioned in the previous chapter, body scans have played a significant role in my meditation journey. Performing body scans by visualizing white light or water flow through my body when I was just a teenager helped me to rest in the present moment, relax enough to calm my mind, and gently fall asleep. A body scan means we scan our body from the toes to the head and bring awareness to every part of the body. We notice any tension, pain, or discomfort, remain present, and breathe into the tensions to release them.[6] The benefits of body scan meditation include stress reduction, increased mental focus, improved sleep, grounding, and enhanced self-compassion.[7]

Now, it's time for you to experience the magic of body scan meditation! You can choose between a more traditional method of body scan or a creative one. Assume a comfortable seating or lying position. For a traditional body scan, you can start scanning the body from the toes up to the head, moving slowly with awareness. If you feel the tension in any body part, you rest there, breathe into the tension, and let it dissolve. Then, once you feel ready, you continue scanning the rest of the body.[8] For a more creative body scan meditation, if you like the idea of wrapping yourself in a ball of white light, I encourage you to visualize this. As you scan the body from toe to head, visualize white, radiant light flowing through your body. You can also visualize water moving through your body. Imagine breathing in healing white light into any place of tension, and then notice what colors and shapes are associated with the tension in your body. As you breathe out, watch the color and shape get pulled out and exit through your nostrils. Do this until you feel the tension is released from the body part. Then, continue scanning your body, breathing in white light into any tension, and with the exhalation, visualize the tension being pulled out of your body through the nostrils. After scanning all body parts, enjoy the relaxation of your entire body. If you find it hard to visualize this, just go with the more traditional method of a body scan. You can do a long practice of body scan meditation, for example, when lying in bed before falling asleep, or a short practice any time during your day.

You can do the body scan meditation with or without sound, depending on your preferences. For my practice, I do body scans in stillness without sound. Some people enjoy using headphones to listen to calming sounds in the background, for example, nature sounds. At night, listening to sounds that honor the darkness, like crickets, frogs, and owls, can help to realign to your natural rhythm. Often, if I feel a particular amount of stress, filling the tub with Epsom salt and hot water with the idea of doing a body scan in the tub is just what is needed. In fact, this is a personal remedy for much of what bothers me. It allows one to relax and uses natural materials to induce a state of well-being and calmness, both physically and mentally. It is self-care, self-nurturing, and an act of self-love that can leave you feeling like a better version of yourself.

PROGRESSIVE MUSCLE RELAXATION

Perhaps you notice, as you go through your days, that the body often feels very tense. For many people, tension has become a part of their everyday reality, and we rarely know what deep relaxation feels like. This is where progressive muscle relaxation comes in. This body scan technique helps you to fully relax your body with two steps. First, you intentionally tense a particular muscle group, such as your hands. Then, you release the tension and become aware of how the body feels genuinely relaxed. Progressive muscle relaxation supports you in lowering the tension and stress levels in your body, reducing anxiety and sleep problems and it can also improve physical symptoms such as headaches.[9] This technique helps you to differentiate between a tense and a relaxed muscle group. This is very important as so many of us only know our body in a tense state. Feeling your body deeply relaxed will make you more aware of the moment when you start tensing your body in your daily life, and you can then interrupt this pattern by intentionally inducing relaxation.

Let's practice! Set aside 15 minutes to do this guided progressive muscle relaxation. Find a comfortable seated position and fully relax. You can also lie down if you are ready to fall asleep. Ground yourself into the surface beneath you and become aware of your natural breathing rhythm. For a few moments, follow your breath as it enters and leaves the nostrils. Bring an overall sense of relaxation to the entire body.

Now, apply tension to a particular muscle group. You can start with your left foot. Inhale deeply and slowly, and tense the muscles of this body part as much as you can for about five seconds. Allow yourself to feel the tension, but be careful not to hurt yourself. You should never feel any pain! After these 5 seconds, release all tension while breathing out. Focus on the difference between the tense and the relaxed body parts. Maintain the relaxation for 15 seconds, then continue with the next muscle group, for example, the left leg. Repeat applying tension and then relaxation. Once you have scanned your entire body in this way, you can rest in a deep, peaceful relaxation.[10] After concluding the meditation, you can take a few moments to contemplate the difference between your body in a state of tension and a state of relaxation. Can you maintain this awareness during your day and bring relaxation to the body?

HOW A BODY SCAN MEDITATION HELPED RELIEVE TENSION

Body scan meditation can be transformational, especially for people with difficulty falling asleep. One example is my student, Paula. She felt very stressed in general, but her biggest challenge was falling asleep. She would create the best sleeping conditions, not using any electronic devices before bed, having only a light dinner, and creating a completely dark, comfortable sleeping environment. As soon as she lay down to sleep, however, the problem began. She felt restless, thinking about the day and getting lost in a storm of thoughts with no end in sight. Counting the breath didn't help, as after a few counts, she was again lost in the racing mind. I suggested that she try a gentle body scan meditation. She opted for the more creative version, visualizing white, calming light flowing through her body, releasing any tension and dissolving it from her body. Initially, it was difficult for her to focus all her attention on her body. As she persisted in the practice, she soon noticed that she felt much more relaxed, and her mind was quieter. After a while, she started to naturally drift into a peaceful sleep during the body scan. She started to incorporate shorter body scans during her day, and soon, she began to feel much more relaxed, joyful, and free.

LOVING-KINDNESS MEDITATION

CULTIVATING COMPASSION

One of the single best benefits of meditation is cultivating compassion for yourself and others. Compassion is defined as being able to feel another's suffering and being motivated to release that person from their suffering.[11] Often, compassion is also referred to as "love in action." Compassion goes beyond just empathy or sympathy because there is an active component to it. Compassion has the motivation and power to transform another person's suffering into love. As such, it is seen as one of the most important qualities to cultivate through meditation. It is said that the Buddha was asked: "Would it be true to say that the cultivation of loving kindness and compassion is part of our practice?" Buddha replied, "No. It would not be true to say that the cultivation of loving kindness and compassion is part of our practice. It would be true to say that the cultivation of loving kindness and compassion is all of our practice." When we look at the current state of our modern world, with all the suffering, high levels of stress, and difficulties maintaining emotional well-being, the words of the Buddha seem relevant now more than ever. Compassion has the potential to transform the problems we face in these times. Practicing compassion opens our hearts to others; it encourages us to take actions based on love and to release the defenses of our ego. As we practice compassion, our barriers and resistances start to soften, and our hearts and minds begin to open. In the Mahayana Buddhist tradition, when a being awakens to a heart full of compassion and wisdom, this is called the "cultivation of bodhicitta." *Bodhi* means "enlightenment," and *citta* means "that which is conscious." The term bodhicitta combines the cultivation of limitless compassion for all beings and the falling away of attachment to our ego.[12]

As we open our hearts to all beings, we are gaining a new perspective of the world. We realize that the world is not for you or against you - it just is. With this comes the understanding that at the end of the day, everyone is doing the best they can from where they are at. This is beautifully expressed by Eckhart Tolle: "If her past were your past, her pain your pain, her level of consciousness your level of consciousness, you would think and act exactly as she does. With this realization comes forgiveness, compassion, and peace." That does not mean we become passive and approve of any harmful actions. A murderer should not be allowed to commit such a cruel act again; it just means that they are at their own level of suffering and mental anguish and far from Source Energy. There are atrocities in this world that are very hard to cultivate compassion for, and I do not say it is easy. What is emphasized here is to cultivate compassion for both the victim and the perpetrator. This reminds me of the story of Akong Tulku Rinpoche, a spiritual master who founded the first Tibetan Buddhist center in the Western world and who was murdered by two men in China.[13] The monks from his Buddhist center in Scotland pleaded with the Chinese government not to give the two men the death penalty, even though they had gruesomely taken away their beloved leader and friend. This symbolizes the deep compassion and love that we can cultivate for all beings, whether we label them as the victim or the perpetrator. Luckily for us, we can start with something easier. For example, having compassion for an aging parent or a co-worker who just got fired and has a family to feed—then turning that compassion inward to us when we mishandle a situation or say something a little too harsh. Once we cultivate compassion for ourselves, we can more easily cultivate it for others.

One powerful practice to cultivate compassion is the practice of Tonglen. In Tibetan, Tonglen means "giving and taking". The practice is a complete surrender of the ego, as we exchange ourselves for others to alleviate their suffering. This method can be applied in daily life, for example, when we are stuck in a traffic jam. Breathe into your heart, and then look around. You will see that other people are as frustrated about being stuck as you are. Then, become more aware of their suffering and feel it, forgetting about your own problem. Breathe in all the negative feelings, and exhale relief and love for yourself and the people around you. Become aware of the perception of oneness arising from your heart and deepen into it.

BENEFITING RELATIONSHIPS

When we think of compassion and relationships, romantic relationships most often come up. However, compassion has an impact on all our relationships. Lending a compassionate ear to a stranger who needs to talk, stopping to help someone in distress, kindly telling the woman in the lady's room that she tucked her skirt into her panties before she left the restroom. Still, since romantic relationships are such a relevant topic for most people, let's take a moment to contemplate how compassion can transform them. Most people enter romantic relationships with what seems like very pure intentions: to love another, to grow, and to create a beautiful life together. More often than not, however, we end up sabotaging relationships and even marriages.[14] According to the American Psychological Association, it is estimated that approximately 40-50% of marriages in the US end in divorce.[15] This seems to be a mirror for all the difficulties we face these modern days in maintaining a peaceful and harmonious relationship with ourselves and others. Researchers found that a fundamental component of cultivating healthy, lasting love is compassion. Being compassionate in our romantic relationships means that we are aware of when our partner is suffering and bring love and kindness towards them.[16] Especially in stressful situations, when negative, unconscious behaviors towards our partner happen more easily, it is essential to cultivate awareness and compassion through meditation practice. And here, it becomes clear again: Meditation is a natural solution, helping to decrease stress and to enhance compassion. With this, meditation is like a healing balm for the people we enter into a relationship with. We can give love more freely, see our partner through the eyes of compassion, and be aware of our triggers and reactions.

One of the most practical ways in which we can use compassion to harmonize any relationship in our life is compassionate communication. Compassionate communication, also referred to as Nonviolent Communication (NVC), is a set of skills that helps us to foster connection and harmony in relationships despite any conflict.[17] It is a practical approach to living based on compassion and love, developed by Marshall Rosenberg. [18] This approach brings our focus back to the root of any conflict: human needs, seeking expression and nurturance within us and others.[19] Whether we are angry at our partner for forgetting our date night or feel frustrated in an argument with a family member – compassionate communication can be applied in any relationship conflict. To apply NVC, we first take a step back from the conflict and return to the present moment. Then, we journey through four components: 1) We observe the situation without judgment. 2) We become aware of our feelings associated with the conflict, separate from all the stories of our mind, and explain how we feel from our perspective. 3) We express our underlying needs that were not met in the conflict. 4) We make a clear request without demand or expectation.

Let's apply this as an example. It is Saturday evening, and your partner wants to pick you up for a romantic date night. You wait. 15 minutes pass. Then 30 minutes... and you are still waiting. You call him, no answer. You start getting worried. Finally, an hour later, he arrives and greets you smilingly, saying he forgot the time as he was chatting with a friend. At this point, you might be angry and frustrated that he kept you waiting for so long for no serious reason. Where usually you would enter a heated argument, you pause. You focus on your breath and return to the present moment. You remember that you just learned compassionate communication and apply it right away. Here is what it could look like: You observe the situation and become aware of your feelings. You realize that you are feeling angry and frustrated because your partner turned up so late and acknowledge these emotions. You then realize that your needs for connection, communication, and safety were not met and that you would like your partner to pick you up on time for the next date.

Then, you communicate this to the other person, for example, by saying: "When you just arrived an hour late to pick me up because you were chatting with a friend, I felt frustrated and angry, as my need for connection, communication, and safety were not met. Would you be willing to make an extra effort to be on time for our next date?" Can you see how there is compassion for both you and your partner, free from judgment, and an intention to bring harmony to the conflict? The power of NVC is that it can be applied to any conflict in a similar way. Are you currently preoccupied with any conflicts in relationships? Now is a great time to practice NVC, and to bring harmony to these conflicts. If we want to bring peace into the world, we first must bring peace into our own lives and especially into our relationships.

A METTA MEDITATION

Now that we have learned so much about the importance of compassion let's bring it all together into a meditation practice. Evoking unconditional love and compassion in meditation is called *metta*. Metta meditation, evoking a "boundless warm-hearted feeling," is part of most meditative traditions in some way. [20] We start the practice of loving-kindness with ourselves and then gradually extend compassion and blessings to those people we love, to those we have a grievance with, and then to all beings. [21] I like to breathe in love and then send it out to different groups of people – to family and friends, and also people in the background who make our lives easier, like the UPS man, grocery store stalkers, truck drivers, and farmers. We can extend our love also to farm animals, ocean life, and all sentient beings on Earth.

Let's have a practice of metta meditation together. Find a comfortable seated position with your spine straight. Take a few deep, slow breaths into your abdomen with long exhalations. Let go of any perceptions of stress and bring relaxation and love to your entire body. Now, bring awareness to the middle of your chest, a little to the right. This is the heart center, known as a portal to love and oneness. You can place one hand on your heart and gently breathe into it to cultivate a connection. For a few minutes, breathe in and out of your heart. (Pause). Open to the feeling of coming back home to yourself, to deepen into intimacy with your own being. From this connection to your heart, begin practicing *metta* towards yourself. While keeping the awareness of your heart, mentally repeat the following phrases: *May I be happy. May I be safe. May I be at peace. May I love myself.* As you repeat these words, you can inhale and exhale love if you feel like it. Let feelings of love, kindness, and warmth arise in your heart. Rest in this state for a few moments. (Pause). Now, visualize a person in your life who you would like to bless. Then, again, repeat the following words: *May you be happy. May you be safe. May you be at peace. May you love yourself.* Focus on the feelings of love, compassion, and kindness in your heart as you repeat these words, and keep visualizing the other person. Rest in this state for a few moments. (Pause). As you deepen the meditation, extend these wishes for happiness, peace, and love to other friends, family members, and strangers. (Pause). Now, bless people who you are in grievances with. (Pause) And finally, extend these wishes of well-being and your loving-kindness to all sentient beings on the planet.

We conclude this *metta* meditation with a poem by Thich Nhat Hanh:

Don't say that I will depart tomorrow —
even today I am still arriving.
Look deeply: every second I am arriving
to be a bud on a Spring branch,
to be a tiny bird, with still-fragile wings,
learning to sing in my new nest,
to be a caterpillar in the heart of a flower,
to be a jewel hiding itself in a stone.

I still arrive, in order to laugh and to cry,
to fear and to hope.
The rhythm of my heart is the birth and death
of all that is alive.
I am the mayfly metamorphosing
on the surface of the river.
And I am the bird
that swoops down to swallow the mayfly.
I am the frog swimming happily
in the clear water of a pond.
And I am the grass-snake
that silently feeds itself on the frog.
I am the child in Uganda, all skin and bones,
my legs as thin as bamboo sticks.
And I am the arms merchant,
selling deadly weapons to Uganda.
I am the twelve-year-old girl,
refugee on a small boat,
who throws herself into the ocean
after being raped by a sea pirate.
And I am the pirate,
my heart not yet capable
of seeing and loving.
I am a member of the politburo,
with plenty of power in my hands.
And I am the man who has to pay
his "debt of blood" to my people
dying slowly in a forced-labor camp.
My joy is like Spring, so warm
it makes flowers bloom all over the Earth.
My pain is like a river of tears,
so vast it fills the four oceans.
Please call me by my true names,

so I can hear all my cries and my laughter at once,
so I can see that my joy and pain are one.
Please call me by my true names,
so I can wake up,
and so the door of my heart
can be left open,
the door of compassion.

— Thich Nhat Hanh, "Call me by my true names"

CHAPTER FOUR
EMOTIONAL WELLBEING: NAVIGATING YOUR INNER WORLD

You are not too emotional. You are not cold-hearted. Odds are you just do not understand what exactly you are supposed to do with your emotions. In modern life, our entire entertainment system is based on outlandish scenarios of emotional unrest and meant to give us, the watchers, some sort of emotional feeling of fright, outrage, romance, or whimsy. Humans are basically raised on it for the most part. But how does that translate into real-world life?

UNDERSTANDING EMOTIONS

THE EMOTION WHEEL

Let's start our journey into the world of emotions by exploring their meaning. In scientific terms, emotions are defined as changes in our being in response to evaluating an inner or outer stimulus that we perceive as relevant to us.[1] This means that emotions are subjective feelings with a specific function to help us evaluate a specific stimulus. There are five different components to emotions: The emotion component, action tendency component, appraisal component, motor component, and physiological component.[2] The emotion component is simply the experience of identifying a feeling, for example, "I am angry." The action tendency component refers to the action of the body after the emotion is identified, for example, "I don't want to be in this situation." In this case, it's an action of withdrawal that might be carried out or not. The appraisal component is the cognitive evaluation of the emotion; we become aware of how the emotion affects ourselves and others. For example, if we are angry, we might appraise the emotion as being threatening to others. The motor component describes how we express emotion, for example, facial expressions like frowning, a change of body posture like our arms, or even raising our voice. The physiological component describes all the chemical reactions in the body that occur in the background of the emotion, for example, the release of the hormone testosterone when we are angry. There are also other factors to consider that determine our emotional response, like gender, culture, and individual dispositions to certain emotional experiences.[3] With about 34,000 distinct emotions known, we can imagine the endless variety of emotional components that can occur for an individual. [4] With so many different emotions, it is no surprise that so many of us feel overwhelmed and don't know what to do with them. Therefore, let's try to simplify it all. Luckily for us, researcher Dr. Plutchik proposed that there are just eight primary emotions that form the basis for all others: joy, sadness, acceptance, disgust, fear, anger, surprise, and anticipation.[5] This conception is widely accepted in the scientific world. It has led to the development of an emotion theory called Plutchik's wheel of emotions, which is meant to simplify the complexity of emotions. For the emotional wheel, the eight primary emotions form the basis as opposites: Joy <-> Sadness, Acceptance <-> Disgust, Fear <-> Anger, Surprise <-> Anticipation.[6] The wheel suggests that these emotions can become milder or intensify. Emotions on the outside of the wheel are milder, whereas emotions at the center are more intense.[7] You can use the emotional wheel as a visual guide to identify what emotion you are feeling. Then, it can help you to understand what might have triggered the emotion, analyze how the emotion connects to other emotions you might experience, and how to take conscious action based on the emotion.[8]

THE LINK BETWEEN THOUGHTS, EMOTIONS, AND BEHAVIOR

Thoughts, emotions, and behaviors are intimately interwoven and hard, if not impossible, to separate or distinguish.[9] Even the statement, "I don't make emotional decisions," involves emotion. It's the *feeling* of emotions not meaning anything and reducing their importance, which can become problematic. In reality, a well-balanced emotional state of being can be our superpower, and emotions are seen as our internal guidance system. Here is why: Often, we find ourselves in the same life situations and repeating the same unwanted behavior over and over again, despite all our attempts to change it. At the root of any behavior are our thoughts and emotions. Our emotions, in the absence of any appraisal or thoughts, can be seen as sensations in the body. For example, sadness can feel like a contraction in the heart, and fear can feel like a knot in our stomach. These feelings accumulate, and we automatically form many different thoughts about them. One emotion can produce thousands of thoughts, which we then experience as overwhelm or confusion.[10] For example, one painful memory of our life, such as a deep regret, can cause us to produce thoughts about the event for many years until we look at the underlying painful feeling.[11] In more scientific terms, in Gray's emotional-cognitive structure theory, emotions are seen as the organizers of thoughts. The theory describes how, over years, emotional nuances lead to stronger emotional patterns, which then form thoughts, expressed as emotional-cognitive structures in the theory.[12] How can we use this knowledge of the connectedness of our emotions and thoughts in everyday life? It invites us to pay more attention to any repeating thoughts we might have, and the emotions which lead to these thoughts. As suggested by somatic therapy approaches, we can then explore these emotions in the body. Often, emotions are "trapped" in the body, often from early childhood experiences that can be perceived as traumatic. [13]

Ultimately, releasing these emotions can free up our thoughts and with that, any unwanted behavior patterns.

Meditation is an essential tool for this exploration. It can provide the awareness, or framework, in which to explore emotions and any feelings in the body more deeply. Usually, our minds are so busy that we don't have the opportunity to just be with our emotions. In meditation, we slow down, cultivate presence, and can take the time to be with any painful emotion. We can cultivate open attention, in which we can observe the emotion lovingly and even allow ourselves to feel it without getting lost in all the thoughts we have formed about the emotion. You might be surprised how quickly unhealthy behavior patterns can change once we address the underlying emotion, which then leads to thoughts and unwanted behavioral responses!

Meditation also gives us the time to rebalance our equilibrium, even if just for a moment.[14] We leave the past where it belongs and permit ourselves to just be here. Be now. Be present. When we allow ourselves to disconnect and just be, the emotional benefits take over. There is no stress. There is no-thing. What a good night's sleep does for the body, good solid meditation practice does for the emotions and sense of well-being. It is a moment to connect with the essence of who we really are without expectation. Meditation has given me permission to be calm and less reactive. To access the stillness and silence that rests within. In a world where reactivity is the norm I often hear people say, "You're so calm and mellow." It's more that I am observing and allowing space for myself and others to just be. In these times of stress and conflict, allowing others just to be as they are, without expectations or judgments, is probably the most beautiful gift we can offer anyone.

EMOTIONAL AWARENESS THROUGH MEDITATION

A friend and student of mine, Anna, used to have a problem with anger. It was small occurrences during the day, small frustrations or arguments with her partner, that would cause a cascade of angry thoughts in her. She couldn't control her anger and even threatened other people physically when in that angry state. Anna is a very sweet and sensitive woman, and when you see her, you would never suspect any anger problem. Even for herself, it's been a mystery how anger could take her over and turn her lovable personality into physical violence. As Anna started to meditate, she practiced a specific exercise. She would evoke the feeling of anger and then rest in the gap between experiencing the emotion and acting on it. As you might know from your personal experience, the emotion of anger can be very strong, and the gap between emotion and reaction is very short. With a lot of meditative practice and awareness, Anna prolonged the gap and was able to rest in stillness. From there, she perceived more spaciousness around the anger. Off her meditation pillow, she saw a drastic change: She stopped reacting based on her anger in the same way she did before. In situations that made her angry, she was able to become aware, take deep breaths, and calm herself. She would leave the situation and only return to the other person once she calmed down. Anna then used the compassionate communication technique described in the previous chapter to express her emotions and her underlying needs and to make requests, all more peacefully and harmoniously. This is the power of a dedicated meditation practice and the willingness to try new ways of relating to ourselves!

MANAGING NEGATIVE EMOTIONS

STRESS AND EMOTIONS

By now, you might see stress as internal, not external. Indeed, stress happens because of the accumulated inner pressure of repressed and suppressed feelings.[15] For example, the more sadness we have accumulated inside of us, the more that sadness gets triggered by external events. The accumulated pressure is looking for relief, and situations in our lives make us feel whatever we have been accumulating inside of us. Related to this, it is important to look at the main three ways we handle emotions: Suppression, expression, and escape. In suppression, we push our feelings away. We deny them and choose not to feel them.[16] This is a conscious process in suppression and an unconscious process in repression. Often, this happens because we don't know what to do with our emotions, and we are afraid to feel them. These suppressed feelings can then lead to tension in the body, cramps, insomnia, and many other somatic conditions related to the experience of stress.[17] In expression, we act on our emotions. This usually feels better than suppression, as part of the energy of the emotion is released. However, expression has some drawbacks, as acting out a negative emotion unconsciously and expressing it towards another person can lead to undesired behavior and relationship problems. Escape means we avoid an emotion by distracting ourselves from it. Have you ever wondered why we have a billion-dollar entertainment industry? Using various forms of entertainment is like a societal-approved method of escaping from emotions we don't want to feel. This is why so many people who feel stressed after a long working day come home and immediately turn on the television. I also know people who live with their radio constantly turned on, as they can't stand the stillness, and with that, facing their emotions.

What, then shall we do with all the emotions to feel less stress and live a more harmonious life? In his book "Letting Go – The Pathway of Surrender," David R. Hawkins describes a mechanism by which we can release the pressure of the emotions we have accumulated. The technique involves becoming aware of a feeling, letting it come up, and staying aware of it. We let the emotion run its course without trying to control it, and we focus on releasing the energy behind the emotion. Essentially, it opens us to the possibility to just be with an emotion and to drop any resistance to feeling it. After a while, you might realize that emotions will come and go, but you are not the emotion – you are the awareness witnessing the emotion.[18] This is where meditation comes in; as we meditate and deepen into the present moment, we can stop identifying with the emotions that pass, and we start to deepen into ourselves as observers. We become more curious about who we really are beyond all the stress and emotional turbulence. And as our meditation deepens, we deepen more into our true Self. We start living in harmony and emotional balance, which is our natural state.

DEALING WITH ANGER AND FRUSTRATION

Let us now look at some common negative feelings and how to deal with them. The best example is probably anger and frustration. We often dramatize them and forget that they are natural emotions, part of the human experience, if they are happening within reason. However, there is such a thing as being addicted to anger or reactivity. Anger is a strong emotion that can trigger the "fight-or-flight" response. The nervous system is in alarm mode; we are very aroused and agitated. The body's stress reaction and the associated thoughts can trap us in a cycle of anger.[19] Meditation helps us to get out of that negative loop by interrupting the unconscious response we have towards anger. We create a gap between the anger and our reaction towards it. One technique that helps with this is called "Being kind with anger." [20] This meditation practice is based on metta meditation, which we explored in a previous chapter.

For the practice, find a comfortable seated posture. Relax your body, and become aware of your natural breathing rhythm. Take a few deep breaths into your abdomen. Start by visualizing a person in front of you towards whom you have positive, kind feelings. Allow yourself to feel love, kindness, and warmth in your heart, and send blessings to the person by mentally saying to them:

Picturing this person, mentally say to them: *May you be happy. May you be safe. May you be at peace. May you love yourself.* (Pause). Now, direct these blessings towards yourself: *May I be happy. May I be safe. May I be at peace. May I love myself.* (Pause). Now, visualize a person you feel angry or frustrated with. Notice any changes in your body or emotional state as you evoke this person. Allow any emotions to come up, observe them, and let them take their course. Stay aware of yourself as the observer. Now, expand your perception of that person. What are their positive characteristics? What are some of their positive actions and contributions? Visualize a sunflower in their heart, and a sunflower in your own heart, symbolizing the love that connects both of you, beyond the anger and frustration. As you keep seeing the other person in front of you, bless them by mentally saying: *May you be happy. May you be safe. May you be at peace. May you love yourself.* (Pause). For a few moments, see if you can find love and kindness in your heart for them. Allow yourself to rest in the echoes of this meditation and to journal on any insights you might have.

EASING ANXIETY AND WORRY

Anxiety and worry are emotional states all of us can relate to. It is known that people who continuously experience a lot of anxiety have difficulties dealing with destructive thoughts that have a lot of power.[21] They tend to get lost in ruminating on negative thoughts and worry in an unproductive way. For these people, it is important to train themselves to think differently. At first, it's a practice of awareness – recognizing when a worrying thought cycle comes up. This is already a big step, as most of the time, we tend to be so identified with negative thoughts that we are not even conscious of them. For example, you might be thinking: "Oh no, I'm stuck in a traffic jam; my boss will fire me if I'm late again. I will lose my job and have no money to pay my rent. I might not find a new job. This is a tragedy." As you start meditating, you might start noticing that thought, and recognizing it for what it is: Just a thought. You might say: "There is this thought again, and I know I used to get lost in it. Now, I choose to think differently and to choose more peaceful and kind thoughts. I'm sure there will be a solution".[22] One technique that can help ease anxiety and worry is a visualization of sitting by a river and seeing your thoughts passing by in the water.[23]

For this practice, imagine you are in a beautiful place in nature, sitting next to a river with glass-clear, crystal-like water. Enjoy the peace and stillness of that space, and allow yourself to relax deeply. Now, start becoming aware of any thoughts you have that cause worry and anxiety. As soon as you become aware of a thought, visualize the thought in the stream of water, slowly flowing with the current away from you. Watch it as it passes by and then disappears. As you become aware of more thoughts, add them to the water and watch them all flow by. If there is an extremely powerful, persistent thought, you can visualize that thought as a rock in the water. Can you notice how the rock blocks the stream of water?

Similarly, keeping this strong thought constantly in your mind blocks the stream of Source energy flowing through you and, with that, well-being and joy. Are you willing to release that thought and let it flow through the water? Continue visualizing your thoughts for as long as you feel like it. Then, connect back to the peace and stillness you feel, and conclude the meditation. You can come back to this practice whenever you feel overwhelmed by anxiety or worry. Find a calm place, take ten minutes, and watch your thoughts flow by in the river.

CULTIVATING POSITIVE EMOTIONS

GRATITUDE AND JOY

An entire book could be written about gratitude. Gratitude is more than just a good feeling – it is the key to a happy life and should be our constant, daily practice. There are two components to gratitude: Firstly, affirming the beauty of life. We say yes to life and acknowledge all the aspects of our lives we appreciate. We affirm the goodness of ourselves and of life. Secondly, gratitude is acknowledging the source of gratitude. We can be grateful for other people, animals, the planet, and even for the universe or Source. This means we recognize the goodness in our life, and then how this goodness is being brought to us.[24] In our modern world, it seems that gratitude has diminished, and states of disappointment, grief, and expectations have made it to the forefront of our busy lives. It doesn't matter how stuck we feel in cycles of negative thoughts or emotions; we can always practice gratitude. On days that you already feel good, gratitude will boost your mood even more, and create a magical day for you. On days that you feel stressed or in a low mood, gratitude can help you to feel more peace, joy, and excitement. Therefore, gratitude is not just a practice for those who already feel happy and grateful – it's a practice for everyone, including those who are prone to a lot of negative emotions. A study conducted among college students who seek mental counseling found that a brief weekly gratitude practice on top of counseling led to greater benefits than counseling alone.[25]

Why is gratitude such a powerful practice? Practicing gratitude can naturally shift our attention away from negative thought patterns and towards more empowered, positive thoughts. Often, negative thoughts distract us from the blessings that are already in our lives; these thoughts are like dark clouds, hiding the sunshine that is always there. As we focus more on the sunshine, the clouds start to be less relevant and then disappear. Gratitude is also a trailblazer for compassion. It clears the forest and makes way for blessing others. Even if we experience conflict with another person, we can always find something to be grateful for about the other person. As we focus more on gratitude and less on any perception of wrongdoings, our relationships blossom and transform. We become more positive towards ourselves and others, and we allow people to be as they are as we see the inherent goodness in them beyond our limited states of mind. Ram Dass puts this into lovely words: *"When you go out into the woods, and you look at trees, you see all these different trees. And some of them are bent, and some of them are straight, and some of them are evergreens, and some of them are whatever. And you look at the tree, and you allow it. You see why it is the way it is. You sort of understand that it didn't get enough light, and so it turned that way. And you don't get all emotional about it. You just allow it. You appreciate the tree. The minute you get near humans, you lose all that. And you are constantly saying, 'You are too this, or I'm too this.' That judgment mind comes in. And so I practice turning people into trees. Which means appreciating them just the way they are."*

As you rest in the echoes of these beautiful words, here are some inspirations on how to integrate gratitude into your daily life:

1. <u>Start the day with gratitude</u>. The moment you wake up and open your eyes, place one hand on your heart and mentally or out loud count ten blessings in your life. Coming up with ten things to be grateful for might seem challenging, but you will find that once you start counting your blessings, you realize there already is an overflow of goodness in your life!

If you still find this practice too challenging, you can start by counting three blessings in the morning. Commit to starting your day with gratitude for one week and observe what happens in your life.

2. Send blessings to the world. As you go through your day, start blessing any people you encounter. The people who clean the streets, the cashier in the supermarket, the waiter in the restaurant, your co-workers, manager, friends, family members, ... You get the idea. Silently or out loud, send blessings and express your gratitude. You can also imagine sprinkling the people with peaceful light or magic dust.

3. Write a gratitude letter. Choose any person in your life and write a letter of gratitude to them. Write what you appreciate about them, how they enrich your life, and how much you love them. You can keep the letter or send it to that person.

4. Go on a gratitude walk. Take yourself on a walk and make gratitude the main focus. Feel gratitude for what you see on your walk, any people you meet, and the ground you walk on. Seeing the world through the eyes of gratitude can dramatically change your perception. It's as if we used to see the world through a grey lens, and then we start seeing the world through a colorful lens. Sometimes, we get so used to our habitual ways of thinking and being that we forget all the beauty around us. On this walk, give yourself the gift of remembering the magic of life!

SELF-COMPASSION AND FORGIVENESS

One of the keys to being at peace with us and others is forgiveness. It matters that you forgive yourself and others. Forgiveness means to release the feeling of resentment against someone. It means setting another person and us free. We have to remember that forgiveness is always for our own benefit. When we forgive, we free ourselves from pain and judgment and from living in the past.[26] Grudges and grievances only hurt the holder. What good will they really do? It is important to explore what forgiveness is not. Forgiving another person doesn't mean we approve of their actions or that we excuse any misbehavior. It also doesn't mean that we have to forgive instantaneously

– it can naturally happen in just one moment, or it can take years. It also doesn't mean that you have to be in contact or in connection with the person you forgave. Just because you forgive someone does not mean you need to hang out with them. You do not need to break bread or see them again. Forgiveness rather means opening up to the notion that everyone is doing the best they can, given the level of consciousness they are at. And with this, to return to peace. Forgiveness is always an expression of the heart, of love. Letting go and coming to a neutral space will open the door to infinite possibilities. Without forgiveness, accessing compassion for yourself or others becomes a daunting task.

Self-compassion is a positive attitude towards us. Three states construe self-compassion: Self-kindness, common humanity, and mindfulness. [27] Self-kindness is about being kind to ourselves when we are in a difficult situation, when we feel like we failed, or when we seem to have no reason to love ourselves. It is a return to knowing that we are inherently worthy, no matter what we have done or what other people say about us. Common humanity means returning to a sense of oneness, to viewing ourselves as part of a broader human experience.[28] It's like we are a wave, finally realizing we are not separate from the ocean of life. Mindfulness, as we explored previously, is observing our thoughts rather than being identified with them. We find a balance of acknowledging our emotions but not being carried away by them. [29] A beautiful practice related to self-compassion is treating ourselves as a friend. If a friend was in a situation you were in or experiencing the problems you have, what would you say to them? How would you behave? Bring this love, kindness, and understanding towards yourself. Hug yourself. Hold yourself in unconditional love and know that you are loved just as you are.

TRANSFORMATION BROUGHT ABOUT BY MEDITATION

When my father committed suicide, it was crushing. Our relationship had been tumultuous at best, and I tried so hard to be his daughter. But after the shock and sadness, anger came. The anger I felt for all his missteps ate away at me... and in my mind, there were a lot of them. The victim inside of me was rearing its ugly head and showing me a side of myself that I did not like. To say I was holding a grudge or a grievance seems light in comparison to what I did feel. Meditation allowed me to forgive and let the pain start to ease. It took me years before I could talk about it without tears. Meditation helped me to peel back the layers and truly feel, heal, and let go. The memory is still there, but now I find myself thinking about the things we enjoyed together—the fun memory snippets instead of the harsh ones. Once I tackled that grudge, I moved on to the next, and so on. Today, I can honestly say there are none. One of the best gifts I ever gave to myself. Freedom from being mad at someone.

CHAPTER FIVE
MEDITATION AND FOCUS ENHANCEMENT

The brain can be likened to a bustling marketplace, teeming with activity and constantly buzzing with various processes. In this intricate neural bazaar, thoughts, memories, and emotions are the diverse goods and commodities on display, each stall representing a unique aspect of cognition. Neurons serve as tireless vendors, communicating through intricate networks, just like merchants haggling and trading in the marketplace. Information flows through synaptic connections, akin to customers moving through crowded lanes, seeking information, or making decisions. Like the marketplace's ability to adapt to changing demands and stimuli, the brain's plasticity allows it to evolve, learn, and adapt over time. Both the marketplace and the brain are dynamic, multifaceted entities brimming with complexity and potential for discovery.

CONCENTRATION MEDITATION

THE ART OF SINGLE-POINT FOCUS

Especially for beginners, it is very typical to be swept away by thoughts during meditation. I remember the first time I meditated many years ago. It was a brief 15-minute meditation, and yet as soon as I sat down and closed my eyes, I felt there were more thoughts than ever before. They tried to pull me in every direction, and soon, I got so distracted by thoughts that I stopped hearing the teacher's instructions. When the meditation came to an end, I realized all I did was think. And yet, I didn't give up after that first chaotic meditation. My first idea was that meditation is too difficult, but I also felt a lot of determination to learn how to quiet all this chatter. Learning how to concentrate the mind and how to single-pointedly focus on an object is a journey. And this often doesn't fit well into our modern world in which we want to achieve everything now, not tomorrow, not next week, but right now. After meditating once, we become discouraged and conclude that we can't meditate, that it just doesn't work for us. On top of that, digitalization has shortened our attention span significantly. Because we live in an instant gratification society, people are often overly optimistic about expectations and results. They get bored very easily when sitting in silence as their mind does not have something to stimulate them and release dopamine.[1] The more we practice coming back to the present moment when our mind wants to go down a rabbit hole or make a list, the easier it becomes. We will notice gaps between thoughts, and this is when meditation becomes more effortless. But we can't skip the first phase of meditation, which is concentration. Even sticking to a routine of consistently meditating just ten minutes a day can significantly increase our attention span.[2]

As a first step, it is essential to develop vigilance, which means seeing and removing distractions. A distraction is any thought, emotion, or sensation that makes us lose our awareness of the present moment. Therefore, if we become aware of a distraction, we find ourselves again in the present moment, and the distraction is not a distraction anymore – rather, it becomes a reminder, a portal back to the present moment. We become friends with the distraction. In general, there are two different forms of distractions: Restless distractions, also called *rajas* in classical texts on meditation, and lethargic distractions, referred to as *tamas*. This means we are usually pulled between a restless, agitated mind and a dull, lethargic mind.

Picture this: You sit in meditation and a lot of thoughts are racing through your mind. Plans for the rest of the day, the argument with your friend, the endless to-do list... You are pulled in every direction. This is an example of a restless state of mind or *rajas*. In contrast to this, you might have meditations in which you almost fall asleep. The mind is dull, unclear, and inert. Perhaps you feel a sense of frustration or apathy and are not very enthusiastic about finishing your meditation. This means you are in a lethargic state of mind or *tamas*. These two mental tendencies can also interact during a single meditation session. When we persist and practice meditation, coming back to awareness again and again, we develop a *sattvic*, or balanced mind.

Let's look a bit closer at how to work with the two main tendencies during meditation: to find a balanced state of mind and a single-pointed focus. For restlessness, it's important to understand why thoughts get power over us during meditation in the first place. If we look at it from a more objective perspective, we will see that all thoughts during meditation can be classified into three categories: Thoughts about the past, thoughts about the future, and thoughts about the present. These thoughts often occur combined with strong emotions that make us grasp at these thoughts. Letting our mind wander has also become a deeply ingrained habit for most of us, and this is reflected in the neural pathways we have created in the brain. Practicing coming back to focus is a great way to exercise the brain, as it creates new neural connections. At first, it takes effort to change the neural pathways in the brain, but the more we practice mindfulness, the easier it becomes. At some point, the same thoughts appear, but we don't react to them, which means they are not a distraction anymore. For lethargy during meditation, we might feel like our mind is blurred and any focus or clarity is lost. An important sign of lethargic distractions is a lack of enthusiasm and aspiration for our meditation practice. Lethargy can occur due to the state of our body, such as feeling tired after not having enough sleep, a crunched meditation posture, meditating in a closed, too-dark space, or having a passive attitude about meditation.

TECHNIQUES TO SHARPEN CONCENTRATION

How, then, do we overcome all these distractions and enhance our concentration? If you are distracted by excitement, recognize this mental tendency and observe it. Apply any technique that helps you – coming back to the breath, visualizing your thoughts as clouds, or reciting a mantra. Stay aware and observe. For lethargy, first, recognize how this distraction shows up for you: Are you sleepy? Unmotivated? Bored? Observe whatever it is that you perceive. Observe how sleepy you are or how bored you are and remain aware. You can also check your posture; make sure the spine is straight, and the shoulders are rolled back. You might want to increase the amount of light in your room or open your eyes slightly. Another beautiful inspiration is to meditate upon joy, enthusiasm, and the beauty of life.

In addition to these internal distractions, there might be external distractions in your environment. Do your best to eliminate any distractions in your environment before meditating, for example, having a private meditation space and keeping your phone hidden from sight.[3] Another way to sharpen concentration is to ensure your body is well taken care of – getting enough sleep, eating a healthy diet, and engaging in physical activity can all support your practice of developing concentration. It can be small changes, such as including more nuts, berries, avocado, or coconut oil into your diet, to provide more healthy fats for the body, which makes it easier to stay focused and concentrate.[4] Meditation is much easier with a body that is balanced and well-nourished. You might also want to connect with nature before meditation, as it can enhance your concentration, make you feel refreshed, and connect you with the beauty of life.

Incorporating these changes can help you in many aspects of your life, not just in your meditation practice. Focus and concentration help us to be more productive, meaning we spend less time on a project as we can focus and get our tasks done. The quality of our relationships improves, as we become a better listener instead of thinking of what we are going to say next. We start speaking with more intention, and more grace.

If you are looking for a specific technique to develop your concentration, you might want to practice fixing your gaze on a specific object for a set time.[5] You first choose an object, for example, a candle flame, a photo of a deity, a flower, or another special object. Make sure it's an object that intrigues you and that you feel enthusiastic about. Sit down in a comfortable meditation position, set a timer for five minutes, and start focusing on your breath. Then, fix your gaze and your entire attention on the object, and let it fully enter your mind. As soon as you become aware that you are being distracted from the object, bring your mind back to focus on the object. Continue practicing like this until the time is over. Then, close your eyes and stay aware of the mental representation of the object. Breathe in and out deeply, and open your eyes when you are ready. This exercise helps to sharpen your mindfulness skills and the ability to train your brain to come back to the present and create new neural pathways.

IMPROVED FOCUS THROUGH MEDITATION

One of my students, Isabel, came to me because she couldn't focus. Whether it was reading a book or working on a project, she couldn't focus longer than 10 minutes on any given task. This started to cause problems, especially in her work life, as she constantly engaged in distractions, which lowered her work performance and led to delayed projects. After about ten minutes into any given task, she couldn't help but give in to whatever impulse presented itself – her phone, checking something on the internet, starting another task, thinking about her day. She then had difficulties focusing again on the task, dropping it and starting a new one, leaving her in a self-created chaos. When we looked a bit deeper, we found that this problem mainly occurred in tasks that Isabel wasn't particularly enthusiastic about. She also didn't like the idea of sitting down on a meditation pillow, closing her eyes, and focusing on her breath. Therefore, we decided to start her meditation practice with an object she was excited about. As Isabel loves nature, she chose her favorite flower as an object for her meditation. Every day in the morning, she sat in her garden, put the timer on for five minutes, and started focusing on the flower, bringing her mind back to the flower whenever she found herself distracted. After a while, she felt so excited about the practice that she extended the time to ten and then fifteen minutes. She also noticed something else: When her mind was quiet and focused on just the flower, a deep inner joy, and calmness started to emerge that felt different than anything she knew before. She started to bring her newfound concentration and inner joy into every task she was doing throughout the day. To her surprise, not only was she able to finally focus for extended periods, but she also felt a lot of enthusiasm for her work and life in general.

MINDFUL PRODUCTIVITY

MINDFUL PRODUCTIVITY – WHAT DOES THAT MEAN?

Usually, when we think of mindfulness, we relate it to presence, slowness, and enjoyment of the present moment. This seems quite contrary to productivity, which we associate with working better and more, achieving goals, and being effective. Traditionally, meditation certainly wasn't designed for people to be more productive. When Buddha sat under the Bodhi tree to become enlightened, he most likely didn't think, "Great, once I'm enlightened, I can finally be more productive and do better at work!" However, times have changed a bit, and in our modern world, productivity appears to be more and more important. Therefore, why not use the benefits of meditation to get better at what we do? Interestingly, increased productivity seems to be a natural by-product of meditation. We know from research that meditation is associated with beneficial changes in brain areas called the prefrontal cortex and right anterior insula.[6] These areas are associated with attention, emotional processing, and cognitive functioning. Thus, meditation can increase our attention span, meaning we can focus longer on a task and better concentrate on it.[7] And it makes sense; if we learn to single-pointedly focus on a candle flame, this enhanced concentration naturally shows up in more areas of our lives. And this is the beauty of meditation: Whatever you do on your cushion, you take with you into the world!

MINDFUL WORK TECHNIQUES

Work is another area in our lives that can be completely transformed by meditation. Research shows that meditation practice is associated with better job performance, higher work engagement, and more job satisfaction.[8] Nevertheless, meditation practice is generally not part of our working day, and rarely do we find an employer who offers meditation classes at work. Still, there is a lot we can do ourselves to reap the benefits of meditation and become more productive and happier at work. After a while, your boss might ask you about your secret for being so motivated and happy, and they might willingly offer meditation classes for everyone! Until then, you can choose to stay consciously present during your working day. For this, make a clear decision as you begin your workday to stay as present as you possibly can.[9] Take a few moments to feel this intention before you start working. Then, during the day, as soon as you become aware that the mind distracts you and makes you wander to think about the argument with your colleague or the date you have after work, you pause. Acknowledge the distraction, but don't go with the story. Bring your attention back to the task you were working on. To help you stay aware, you can also practice meditation at work. Most likely, there won't be time for a 30-minute meditation practice. However, just five or ten minutes of your favorite breathing technique can do wonders! Another very effective technique is to create reminders to stay present. This can be little notes in your office, a reminder on your phone, or even a colleague who shares the practice of staying aware with you. Another mindful work technique is to stop multitasking. This might seem challenging as multitasking has become the new normal. You can disrupt this pattern by choosing to do exactly one thing at a time. You might be surprised how much more productive you are as a single-tasker![10] This relates to improving time management at work. You can schedule similar activities at the same time, batch tasks, and schedule short breaks for mindfulness exercises.

Most importantly, whatever happens during the working day and whatever distractions you encounter, you can make them your friends and let them guide you back to the present moment.

HOW MEDITATION IMPROVES PRODUCTIVITY

A while ago, I had a conversation with my friend Mary. She told me that she had just started a new job – in fact, it was her third new job this year! As I inquired about her reason for changing jobs so frequently, she explained to me that after a few weeks of starting a new job with excitement, her enthusiasm dropped. She wouldn't finish her tasks, lose focus, come late to work, and miss deadlines. To my surprise, Mary believed that the reason for her loss of enthusiasm and shift into unproductivity was due to the jobs, not because of herself. She didn't see that it was her inner world, her tendencies, that created this situation. I knew that meditation would help her to find back to both her enthusiasm and productivity, no matter what job she was in. We developed a meditation practice that worked well for her, focusing first on her breath to calm her mind, and then bringing this concentration to her workplace. A few weeks after starting her meditation practice, Mary called me to say that she had a transformative insight. For the first time, she was able to observe her thoughts, and she saw all the negative thought tendencies about herself and the job, and the way she distracted herself from her work tasks. This awareness is indeed the most important step, as we can only change what we are aware of. She integrated short meditations into her working day – either focusing on her heart to access her inner enthusiasm or box breathing to increase her focus. It didn't take long before her productivity at work improved a lot. But she didn't just break the cycle of quitting her job- she felt happier and freer in every area of her life and performed better at her job because she felt motivation and an inner drive to perform well.

OVERCOMING DIGITAL DISTRACTIONS

THE IMPACT OF TECHNOLOGY ON FOCUS

It's no secret that modern technology is a powerful distraction. Digital distraction is a big deal - people now walk down the street or through the store looking down at their phones, running into things, or getting run over as they are not paying attention. Even children are at risk of a decline in cognitive function and mental health due to consuming digital media.[11] Looking at the neurobiology of digital distraction, we know that every time we check our phones, dopamine is released in the brain.[12] Our brain is looking for more dopamine; to get it, we again check our phone for the hundredth time in a day. This means we can easily become addicted to technology, and we must be quite firm in overcoming digital distractions. One of my friends just shared with me that to help her with digital distractions, she shuts her computer off totally at the end of the workday, as she works from home. Additionally, she has a metal box that she puts her phone into. She has also removed email and social media shortcuts from her phone. This is an example of the firmness we need in this digital age to free ourselves from distractions. The best thing we can do is to shut down our phones and laptops whenever we don't use them, and if we are still distracted, to lock them away. Another problem with technology is that checking our phones and the content we see can trigger the "fight-or-flight" response and the release of cortisol. This means that on top of all the stressors we inevitably encounter in our daily lives, we have an additional stressor constantly in our pockets. The consequence can be stress-related symptoms such as anxiety, sleeping problems, and even chronic disease.[13]

MINDFUL TECH USAGE

Are you motivated to overcome these digital distractions? As we can't lock technology away for the rest of our lives, we must find a way to deal with it more mindfully. You can set an intention to use all digital appliances with mindfulness. This includes all screen time, TV, watches with notifications, and the computer besides the ever-distracting smartphone. The first and easiest thing you can do is to turn off all notifications. We underestimate the impact of being constantly reminded to check our phones, messages, and social media. As you turn off the notifications, at the same time, you can turn on your phone's screen time tracker to get an idea of how much time you spend on your phone. This warrants a warning, as for most of us, our screen time is higher than expected, which can serve as a motivation to become more mindful of our technology usage.

In a similar vein, giving yourself a break from digital information and engaging in thoughts and ideas outside of the technological realm can bring new inspiration and relaxation to your body. A much-needed break from the light emanating from your screen. This kind of activity in the "real" world allows the brain to give more attention to what is right in front of it - like we used to do before the smartphone and computer screen era. It is recommended to choose one day of the week during which you put your phone and laptop away and spend 24 hours without any technology.[14] This might sound challenging, but after an initial period of discomfort, it brings so much freedom – being in the moment, undisturbed, and remembering the beauty of life and connections with other people beyond WhatsApp and Facetime. If you are ready to take this experiment one step further, you can spend an entire weekend, week, or month away from the digital realm. This allows your nervous system to reset, and you can connect more deeply with yourself again.

REGAIN CONTROL OVER DIGITAL DISTRACTIONS

A student of mine, Laura, asked me for advice as she felt it was impossible to become free from her digital distractions. She was self-employed, owned a business, and was working and available for client calls 12 hours a day. This means she was constantly on her phone and laptop, answering queries, emails, and calls about her products. On top of that, social media played an important part in her work as she used several platforms to promote her services. I think you get the picture – rarely a moment passed that she wasn't preoccupied with the digital world. What Laura needed of course, was set working hours and clear boundaries with clients. What she needed even more was meditation – a daily practice of being just with herself. After a few weeks of meditating, Laura realized that all the digital distractions she had created and entertained were distracting her from being with herself. She noticed how uncomfortable she felt, sitting in silence without being able to take a call or answer a message. She had to face her thoughts, emotions, and reasons for letting technology control her. After a while, as she became more comfortable with the silence and herself, she didn't feel a need any longer to spend her days in the digital realm. She outsourced most of the digital part of her work to a virtual assistant, which freed her time to allow her creativity to flow again and to create more products and services. Her business blossomed as a result. Laura believed that it was only through meditation that she was able to free herself from all the digital distractions and create a life she loved.

MAKE A DIFFERENCE WITH YOUR REVIEW!
Unlock the power of generosity...

"Just as ripples spread out when a single pebble is dropped into water, the actions of individuals can have far-reaching effects." – His Holiness the Dalai Lama

Hey there!

We hope you've been enjoying learning more about the world of meditation with **"Meditation for The Modern Mind: A Beginners Guide to Stress Relief and Emotional Well-Being"** *by B.M. Wolf.* Your thoughts and opinions matter to us, and we'd love to hear what you think about the book!

Your review can make a big difference. It not only helps fellow readers decide if this book is right for them but also supports the author in their mission to spread the benefits of meditation far and wide.

Remember, just like a ripple in a pond, your review has the power to touch lives beyond your own. So, why not take a moment to share your thoughts and experiences with others?

Spread the joy of mindfulness and self-discovery by leaving a review today. Together, let's unlock the power of generosity and make a positive impact in the world, one review at a time.

64

Thank you for being a part of our community and for your support in promoting peace, calm, and emotional wellness through the pages of "Meditation for the Modern Mind."

With much gratitude,

— *B.M. Wolf*

NAMASTE

CHAPTER SIX
DEEPENING YOUR MEDITATION PRACTICE

How do goals and experiences vary as one progresses through the stages of meditation? Something that is often shared by meditators is: "I'm not doing this right." As mentioned before, this is a common myth about meditation. But why would one think this? Their human mind is comparing themselves to someone else and perceiving that the other person is doing it right. When the reality is, it might just look like the image of a perfect meditation. We do not know what someone else is going through in their practice. What challenges are they currently trying to overcome, successfully or unsuccessfully? When starting anything new, or beginning to go deeper, and trying a new technique... it's ok to start messy. It's okay not to have all the things like the perfect cushion, the perfect space with all the perfect décor. Meditation is a space to just be you. No competition, no expectations, no assumptions. It reminds me of The Four Agreements by Don Miguel Ruiz. 1. Always do your best. 2. Be impeccable with your words. 3. Do not make assumptions. 4. Do not take anything personally. Have acceptance at the moment about where you are without any comparison or self-criticism.

PROGRESSION IN MEDITATION

THE FOUR STAGES OF MEDITATION

It's time to explore the different phases of our meditation journey - how to master the different stages and overcome any roadblocks. In Tibetan Buddhism, there is a famous 3000-year-old parable that describes the journey of a meditator to attain "calm abiding", known as *Samatha*. In the story, as the student begins her journey and starts a meditation practice, she begins ascending a mountain together with a monkey and an elephant. The elephant symbolizes the human mind, and the monkey stands for distraction.[1] Both the elephant and monkey are pictured in dark colors, symbolizing the hindrances of the mind and unfocused attention. At the beginning, the monkey (distraction) is dragging the elephant (our mind) on a leash, leading it into chaos. As the student starts meditating and walks up the mountain, she uses tools such as rope, the intention to calm the mind, and fire, representing effort. After a while, the elephant and the monkey begin to slow down as the meditator starts gaining control over them, and their color becomes lighter. Eventually, the tools are put aside, as effort is no longer required – calmness of the mind has become natural. As the meditator reaches the top of the mountain, the monkey has disappeared and she rides on the elephant holding a sword, representing wisdom. *Samatha*, calm abiding, is reached, and the next journey into *Vipassana*, insight, begins.[2] Let's look at the four stages to reach *Samatha* in more detail.

STAGE 1: ESTABLISHING A MEDITATION PRACTICE

You enter the path of meditation and start chasing the elephant, who in turn is chasing the monkey. In its essence, stage one is very simple: All you have to do is meditate. It doesn't matter if there are thousands of thoughts distracting you; you keep meditating. As mentioned previously, this first part of the journey can also be the most challenging: We are dealing with our scattered monkey mind. It seems impossible to control our minds. Therefore, the monkey and elephant are colored in black; they are obstacles. A lot of fire, or effort, is required to calm down the elephant and monkey. In this first stage, it is important to have consistent daily practice and to develop determination. The clearer your intention for practicing meditation, the stronger your determination, and the easier the journey. This might be a good time to revisit chapter one about setting up your meditation space and knowing your why. This first stage isn't about doing it perfectly but about doing the best we can. The goal of stage one is to set a clear intention for your meditation practice that fuels your inner fire and to develop a daily meditation practice.

STAGE 2: OVERCOMING DISTRACTIONS

After practicing meditation for a while, you might find that you are still trying to catch the elephant, but both the elephant and monkey have slowed down. Their color starts turning from black to white, symbolizing that the first obstacles to meditation were overcome, and the periods of being lost in the chaos of the mind are shorter. And so... You sit down for your meditation practice every day, observing your breath, and yet you still find yourself lost in thoughts. You have encountered the strongest roadblock on the path: Mind-wandering.[3] You encounter a distracting thought, forget the object of your meditation, and drift off into the stories of the mind. As mentioned in the previous chapter, our task is to become aware of any distractions and to return to our object of meditation. Again, this means that the distractions in themselves are not the problem; what happens afterward is what matters – do we forget and wander off into the stories of our mind, or do we become aware and refocus our attention on our breath? Whatever happens, the practice is to remain kind and loving to ourselves. We don't want this stage to be rigid or forceful. Yes, we do need some determination, but let's not forget the real meaning of meditation: To get to know ourselves and to love ourselves in-depth. Let love be a guiding force; find back the joy of sitting with yourself, whether the monkey mind is active or not. At the end of stage two, you will find that the periods of mind-wandering are shorter, and the periods of sustained focus on the object of meditation are longer.

STAGE 3: EXTENDED ATTENTION AND REMEMBRANCE

By now, you have got a taste of the magic of meditation. There is still effort in calming the mind, but periods of mind-wandering are much shorter. There are longer phases of being focused on the object of meditation. However, in the parable, a rabbit appears on the back of the elephant, symbolizing new obstacles: Drowsiness and sleep. In the first two stages, excitement was the main distraction, and now, we start to get to know lethargic distractions. You might be focused on your breath but notice unclarity and dullness, a sense of passivity and loss of enthusiasm. It can be helpful to explore new meditation postures, to try a standing position, and to make sure that you get enough sleep and exercise. We can also find new objects of meditation: If we are used to the breath or a candle flame, we can now focus on the heart as our object, letting enthusiasm, bliss, and love radiate from it. The secret to making it through this stage is to keep the inner fire alive, to infuse our daily practice with joy and determination. As Rumi said: "It is burning of the heart I want; this burning, which is everything. More precious than a worldly empire." At the end of this third stage you will be able to differentiate between exciting and lethargic distractions, be aware of when they arise, and know how to overcome them.

STAGE 4: CONTINUOUS REMEMBRANCE

Meditation becomes more natural and requires less effort. There are longer gaps between thoughts, in which we dive into stillness and the real depth of meditation. By now, you will know that this whole journey is not about forcing or making all thoughts go away; it's about awareness. Staying mindful. Coming back to the present moment again and again, and witnessing distractions rather than getting lost in them. We can now differentiate between gross and subtle distractions.[4] A subtle distraction means that you remain aware of the object of meditation, but for a short moment, there is a distraction passing by. With gross distractions, the focus on the breath remains in the background, but a mental distraction comes to the forefront. As the elephant and monkey get quieter and quieter, they'll come up with more subtle ways of distracting you. Here is where you can apply all that you learned in the last stages: To note and remain aware. We see the distraction, allow it, and accept it, and yet, we don't get lost in it. The goal of stage four is to overcome gross distractions.

BEYOND THE STAGES

While the parable and the stages can be a helpful framework, they are not linear. They overlap, intertwine, and cross over. We might find ourselves in stage four during one practice, and the next day, we are back in stage one. We are all on our journeys, and it's important to follow our inner guidance. Sometimes, especially when meditation seems effortful, it can be good to remember that every meditator started by chasing the elephant and monkey. The best thing we can do is to make sure we enjoy the journey up the mountain, no matter what stage we are at.

CHALLENGES AND BREAKTHROUGHS

Some of the common challenges on the meditation journey are that the mind doesn't seem to quiet down; the chatter will not stop. On top of that, we get distracted by sounds or physical sensations. We start feeling fidgety or getting the "itchies". The thought arises that we are meditating in the wrong way. And then there are all these expectations that something is "supposed" to happen. And didn't this one teacher say there was a higher state called *samadhi*, in which there are no thoughts? While trying to reach higher states of meditation, the ego might then guide us down a path of... "I'm better than others because I'm spiritual." This is not the case – meditation is about realizing oneness and that in essence, we are all the same. Another common challenge of meditation is that "I don't have the time." The bottom line is, we make time for what is important to us. If lowered stress, blood pressure, and heart rate variability are important enough to you, I guess that the time will be found easily and effortlessly, just like with anything else. People often start with just 5 – 10 minutes a day and gradually add more time in. Add a minute every week or two until you get to the desired amount of time.

With all these challenges happening while sitting on your meditation pillow and practicing day after day, the true benefits of meditation show up while you are engaged with the world. New, subtle nuances appear to help you realize that a better version of yourself is starting to reveal itself. The way you view yourself and the world might shift. Your heart opens, and you start seeing the world through the eyes of love, rather than the eyes of your personality. Often, it is only by noticing how situations that used to be stressful are not triggering us so much anymore, that we notice the benefits of our practice. We become calmer, more joyful, and more loving with ourselves and others.

Beyond all these challenges, we meditate to find ourselves in the space in between our thoughts, where our mind is fully present and not wandering down all the rabbit holes that lead us nowhere. Sometimes, that happens for a millisecond; at other times it can happen for an indistinguishable amount of time. Until you eventually reach a point of staying in "the gap" for as long as you like. The gap is a direct connection to the Source of all life, the infinite awareness of being, unlimited creativity, and deep stillness.[5] This gap can only occur beyond the mind, beyond any labels. As soon as your mind recognizes that you are in the gap, you are no longer in it. In fact, you will not know you are in the gap until afterward when you say to yourself, "Whoa...that was deep".

There is a very powerful technique that can help both with distractions and extending the gap, which is becoming aware of the pauses after inhalation and exhalation. For this, you sit down in a comfortable meditation posture and close your eyes. Become aware of your natural breathing rhythm. After a while, notice short, natural pauses of around one second after each inhalation and after each exhalation. Focus your attention on these pauses. It's not about holding the breath or inducing the pause but finding the pause that is always there. After each inhalation, rest in the pause, and after each exhalation, rest in the pause. Each pause is a small gap between thoughts, a moment of stillness. Eventually, these pauses will get longer and longer until you are in the gap, and breathing happens naturally without effort.

71

A PERSONAL JOURNEY OF GROWTH IN MEDITATION

Before a consistent meditation practice, something that was an unwelcome challenge was being defensive and building an emotional wall around myself. Getting to the point of being so shut down that a significant other would say something to me like, "You are so rigid and cold." I just did not know how to process, how to work through what just happened, and how to truly express myself. Part of this came from a case of people pleasing and living up to other people's ideals, which then compromised what I wanted and took my voice away. A consistent practice of meditation helped me to heal from trauma, peel back the layers of conditioning, and find myself again. Kind of like Robin Williams in the movie "Hook," when he reconnects to his alter ego of Peter Pan. He remembers who he is, and the layers of conditioning melt away, revealing a more joyful, authentic, and intentional version of himself. Today, my defenses are low, and my acceptance is high. Compassion has grown immensely; even though I was already a compassionate person, I find that it is an area of my life that constantly grows and gets better. Frustration is no longer a normal state of being - now there is acceptance. I can express my desires and boundaries without the guilt of letting someone down. Basically, I am owning and can express what works for me and what doesn't work for me in a gentle, kind, and loving way.

ADVANCED MEDITATION TECHNIQUES

VIPASSANA AND INSIGHT MEDITATION

In the parable we looked at, the path is leading towards *Samatha*, calm abiding. This means a practitioner has stabilized in awareness; the mind can remain calm and concentrated on an object. In some traditions, this is considered the starting point of meditation. Because to enter the gap of meditation, the mind has to be quiet. Then, we are ready for the next journey, the one of insight, Vipassana, also known as Insight meditation. It's good to gain an understanding of *Vipassana* meditation as it's more of an approach to meditation instead of a specific type of meditation. *Vipassana* is a Sanskrit term meaning "to see things as they really are." [6] It is said that Vipassana meditation has descended directly from the Buddha himself. In the first stage of Vipassana, the mind is trained in *Samatha*, to remain calm and in the present moment. Once *Samatha* is stabilized, the practitioner begins with Insight meditation. In Insight meditation, there is no object of meditation, such as the breath. The focus is on deepening into pure awareness, the gap between thoughts. As you rest in awareness, you start to realize that you are not just thoughts, emotions, and personality.[7] You are the awareness beyond it all. Everything keeps changing in the inner and outer world, and yet, something never changes awareness, the Self. In modern Vipassana retreats, students are encouraged to sit in the same position for long periods, even if pain arises. This can be helpful for some students and not for others. I'm a big fan of "comfort is queen," and there is something for everyone when it comes to meditation. The concept of letting go of suffering, or as I like to call it, "emotional freedom", can only benefit whoever chooses to embrace it.

CHAKRA MEDITATION

Chakra meditation is something that I could go on and on about for days, but there is not nearly enough room in this one book for all of that. Seven main chakras tend to be the "agreed" upon chakras. *Chakra* is a Sanskrit word that translates to wheel or circle. In the most basic of terms, chakras are energy points within the body situated along the spine.[8] Each chakra correlates with organs, emotions, energies, and specific qualities. Think of feelings and expressions such as, "I have butterflies in my stomach" or "I have a lump in my throat." Yup, that is your chakra sharing information with you. There are many energy points, but for beginners or those just getting into chakras overall, start with the seven main chakras.[9]

1. **Muladhara Chakra:** The Root Chakra is located at the base of the spine, in the general area of the perineum. It is characterized by the emotions of survival, stability, ambition, and self-sufficiency. There is a connection to the Earth element and an association with the color red. An unbalanced root chakra can lead to feelings of being ungrounded and not

belonging, lack of enthusiasm and purpose, insecurity, and frustration. A balanced root chakra can result in confidence, stability, feeling grounded, vitality, and inner strength.

2. **Svadhishthana Chakra:** The Sacral Chakra is situated in the lower abdomen. It's related to sexual energy, as well as creativity, emotions, and self-worth. It's related to the water element and the color orange. An unbalanced sacral chakra can result in emotional instability, irritation, lack of creativity, and difficulties with sexual energies. In its balanced state, the sacral chakra leads to a vibrant, happy, positive state, to a connection with our intuition and compassion.

3. **Manipura Chakra:** The Solar Plexus Chakra is situated in the navel area. It's connected to self-confidence and self-esteem, the experience of ourselves as an individual, and the flow of our life force energy. This chakra is connected to the fire element and the color yellow. An unbalanced solar plexus chakra can result in anger issues, digestive problems, depression, and a lack of self-esteem. In its balanced state, the solar plexus chakra helps us to feel energetic, confident in ourselves, and to be productive.

4. **Anahata Chakra:** The Heart Chakra is situated in the heart area. It's connected to love, compassion, trust, passion, and devotion. We can associate this chakra with the air element and green color. An unbalanced heart chakra can lead to a lack of trust, moodiness, anxiety, jealousy, and fear. In a balanced state, the heart chakra opens us to harmony, unconditional love, compassion, and kindness.

5. **Vishudda Chakra:** The Throat Chakra is located in the throat area. Its qualities are spiritual aspiration, purity, healthy self-expression, and communication. Vishudda Chakra relates to the ether element and blue color. An unbalanced throat chakra can result in quietness, an inability to express oneself, and a feeling of weakness. In its balanced state, the throat chakra symbolizes healthy self-expression, spiritual insight, creativity, and great communication.

6. **Ajna Chakra:** The Third Eye Chakra is in the middle of the forehead between the eyebrows. Its qualities are intelligence, clarity, insight, and

self-knowledge. This chakra is associated with the color indigo. If the third eye chakra is unbalanced, this can result in physical symptoms such as headaches or blurry vision and unclarity, mental confusion, or weakness. In its balanced state, the third eye chakra makes us feel vibrant and confident, clear, connected with our intuition, and free from material attachments.

7. **Sahasrara Chakra:** The Crown Chakra is situated on the top of the head. Its associated color is violet. Sahasrara Chakra symbolizes enlightenment, universal wisdom, and cosmic consciousness. If the crown chakra is imbalanced, there might be a sense of frustration, melancholy, and emotional imbalance. When balanced, the crown chakra opens us up to spiritual insight, inner peace, and seeing the world for what it truly is.

Meditating on chakras can be as simple as envisioning the color of the chakra and breathing into it. Bring your attention to the area of the chakra while taking several long slow deep breaths in.

Let's dive into the practice of chakra meditation. Read through this and then give it a try for just a few minutes. Sit in a comfortable position and start by taking several long slow deep breaths in. Once you feel ready, bring your attention to your root chakra, also known as your Muladhara chakra. It is located near your tailbone or at your perineum. See where your attention goes naturally; this is a good place to start. As you bring your attention there, envision a deep ruby-red color at your root chakra and breathe into the space. Take several long slow deep breaths in and release just as slowly through your nose. As you breathe, continue to observe the ruby red color and see it expand or contract to be within a few feet of your body. Feel the energy in your lower body and your root chakra. As you get ready to finish up, continue to breathe and let the stillness and silence settle in. Whenever you are ready, you can gently open your eyes. What did you feel during the practice? What do you feel afterward? The root chakra helps us to stay grounded, and when working with chakras, it is good to start here first. Working on an upper chakra without first making sure your lower chakras are balanced can have undesirable results. A seven-chakra meditation is a great way to realign the chakra system and bring yourself to the present moment. Based on the list above, you can also see what chakra you feel drawn to work with.

THE TRANSFORMATIVE POWER OF ADVANCED MEDITATION TECHNIQUES

It is important to consider that many people believe meditation is just about quieting the mind. It is still not very well known that meditation, in essence, is about insight into who we truly are. One of my students was working with the breath for four years, not knowing that there was more to meditation than focusing on an object. When I introduced some advanced meditation techniques, her life changed. Her mind was already prepared for deeper stages of meditation, and very soon she found herself in the gap for extended periods. With this deepening and insight into her being, she became a yoga and meditation teacher herself.

MAINTAINING CONSISTENCY

OVERCOMING PLATEAUS

Encountering plateaus on our meditation journey happens to all of us. After a while, the mind quiets down; we stay with the breath for minutes, not seconds. It can feel like our meditation is not progressing further – as if we are stuck. At least we are stuck in a peaceful place. But there are some tricks to continue the ascend onto the mountain. Firstly, we have to keep in mind that the subtle benefits of meditation practice reveal themselves as we engage with the world. We meditate for ourselves, and we meditate for others. It can take some time for the benefits and changes to be reflected in the world.

Still, if you feel you have reached a plateau in your practice, you might feel like you don't know how to go deeper into meditation.[10] In this case, it is important to understand that we don't necessarily need to know, as deeper states of meditation happen beyond the knowingness of the mind. You can transition into resting awareness meditations and start focusing your attention on the awareness itself. This means you, your awareness, become the object of meditation. This meditation technique is called self-inquiry and was suggested by a great Indian sage called Ramana Maharshi. For this, after quieting the mind, start evoking the question, "Who am I?". Don't try to answer this question, but let the stillness be the answer and take you deeper into awareness. This question opens you up to who you are beyond thoughts, labels, and personality. Ramana Maharshi said: "The question 'Who am I?' is not really meant to get an answer, the question 'Who am I?' is meant to dissolve the questioner." The question dissolves the mind, our personal self and deepens us into the insight stage of meditation, to deepen into who we really are, in essence.

Another way to navigate plateaus is to drop any goal we might have and to focus on what we have cultivated so far: Being present. Being aware and available. When staying in the present moment without any grasping, meditation deepens automatically. At some point, we must drop any effort, any sense of doing, and deepen into beingness.

Regardless of where you are at in your meditation journey, it can be very supportive to get to know other meditators [11] – you can look for group meditations in your city or online, use the live class feature of the Insight Timer app, or even attend a meditation retreat.

One very important note at this point: Spiritual bypassing is a thing, especially in today's modern world with all the tendencies to distract ourselves from us. It is an illusion to believe that with meditation, our life will be perfect, and there will never be any difficulties again. The Buddha affirmed thousands of years ago that life in this human form means there will always be suffering, by making it one of the four noble truths of Buddhism.[12] Meditation invites us into a new perspective – not hiding or escaping but seeing, embracing, and loving everything. If you find yourself meditating to not be with your problems, or if you are very detached and don't allow yourself to feel your emotions, chances are you might bypass yourself. In this case, emphasize love and compassion for yourself in every practice, and allow yourself to feel everything.

RITUALIZE YOUR PRACTICE

When we make something a ritual it becomes part of our life.[13] Like our bedtime ritual. Or our getting ready for work ritual. In our lives, we would never skip getting ready for work and just roll out of bed and be there with our unbrushed teeth, messy hair, and sleep clothes. Unless you work from home, then you often get ready from the waist up. Meditation is just like brushing your teeth. When I get up in the morning, I go pee. Let my dogs go pee... then feed them. Then I meditate. My teacher refers to this as "R.P.M."-Rise. Pee. Meditate. After meditation, I exercise for just a few minutes. It is my daily ritual. It is how I start my day. Just like for coffee drinkers, if they do not get a cup of coffee their day is off. It has become their ritual. It has been scientifically proven that what you do in the first hour of your day sets the tone for the rest to come after. Meditation sets that tone.

Therefore, the invitation is to ritualize your practice. Just like exercise or eating right, doing it occasionally will effectively do nothing for your body. Meditation is the same thing, "crisis meditation" or only meditating on the weekends when you have time, will not have as much of an impact as a consistent practice.[14] It is about committing ourselves to staying consistent with our practice. Maybe you know the saying "How you do anything is how you do everything." How we show up for our meditation practice is exactly how we show up in our lives. And at some point, your entire day and life will become a ritual, as we can turn everything in this life, even the most mundane moments, into a sacred ceremony.

THE IMPORTANCE OF CONSISTENCY IN A MEDITATION PRACTICE

One of my students lives at a meditation center for most of the year, and occasionally returns to her home country for 2 or 3 months, to see her family and friends. She observed that while living at the meditation school, she would meditate for several hours every day. Then, back home, she would keep this up for a week. Then she started meditating every second day... Then once a week... And soon she found herself only doing the famous "crisis meditations". It took her a lot of determination to eventually keep up her meditation practice of one hour every day, no matter where she was. Sometimes, we have to make a firm commitment to ourselves and apply meditation in our daily lives: becoming aware of all the thoughts that tell us today is not a good day to meditate, it's too hard to meditate at home, there is no time, ... Once we give in, chances are we keep making excuses. As we see, this can happen even to advanced meditators.

CHAPTER SEVEN
BETTER SLEEP, BETTER LIFE

In today's modern world, with all the stressors, pressure, and busyness, it's no wonder why sleep deprivation is at an all-time high. Researchers have identified insufficient sleep as a global public health problem, with high costs for both individuals and society at large.[1] Sleep deprivation can cause a weakened immune system, puts your body at a higher risk for disease, as well as having a cognitive impact. In fact, driving while sleep-deprived is just as dangerous as someone driving under the influence of substances.[2] Insufficient sleep has been associated with 7 of the 15 leading causes of death in the United States, such as cardiovascular disease, diabetes, accidents, and hypertension.[3] Sleep deprivation can become a negative cycle that isn't easy to break. It is estimated that 18% of adults in the US have used sleep medication at some point in their lives.[4] Meditation can act as a natural sleeping aid. Practicing meditation can help you with all aspects of sleep: Addressing patterns that prevent you from sleeping well and supporting you with falling and staying asleep. Meditation is also a powerful way to both start and end your day.

SLEEP DISORDERS AND MEDITATION

UNDERSTANDING SLEEP DISORDERS

Sleep disorders are conditions that interfere with our ability to have a healthy amount of high-quality sleep. [5] They impact the quality, duration, and timing of sleep. More than 50 million people in the US are known to have a sleep disorder. In today's world with all the stressors and worries, many more people experience problems with their sleep without an official diagnosis. There are some signs to recognize a sleeping disorder: You have problems with your sleep regularly, and it becomes more challenging to perform your daily activities. You might experience excessive tiredness during the day, although you got a healthy amount of sleep the night before. [6] You might have difficulties falling asleep, difficulties staying asleep, or find it challenging to wake up in the morning. [7] There are over 80 known sleep disorders to be differentiated, with the most common ones being insomnia, restless legs syndrome, narcolepsy, and sleep apnoea. [8] Insomnia means that an individual has problems falling asleep or staying asleep each night. Acute insomnia refers to sleeping problems lasting one night or a few weeks, whereas chronic insomnia lasts for three days a week for three months or more. [9] Restless legs syndrome refers to a neurological disorder in which an individual feels an irresistible urge to move their legs when falling asleep, while sleeping, or during the day. Narcolepsy describes a condition in which a person has difficulties regulating their sleep pattern, which can lead to excessive tiredness during the day. People with a condition of sleep apnoea have a disrupted sleeping pattern caused by moments in which they don't breathe while sleeping. [10] Causes of sleeping disorders include hormonal imbalances in the body, neurological issues in the brain, genetic predisposition, side effects of medication, substance use, using digital devices before bedtime, medical conditions, and mental health conditions.[11] Additionally, experiencing stress or working late hours are risk factors for developing sleeping disorders. Traditionally, sleeping disorders are treated with cognitive behavioral therapy, medication like the well-known sleeping pills, and supplements like melatonin.

MEDITATION AS A SLEEP AID

Scientific studies have shown that meditation is an alternative, effective treatment option for adults who suffer from chronic insomnia. [12] In one study, patients diagnosed with chronic insomnia who took part in an 8-week mindfulness meditation course showed fewer symptoms of insomnia, compared to patients who didn't meditate. In another study, people with chronic insomnia who practiced heartfulness meditation for eight weeks showed a significant improvement in their condition. [13] These are just two examples of a large body of scientific research that emphasizes the benefits of meditation for sleep disorders. Why is it that meditation seems to be an effective, natural sleep aid? Scientists found that meditation decreases psychological and physiological arousal before sleep, and disturbances during sleep, which are important predictors of insomnia. [14] This is not surprising, given that meditation is well-known to reduce stress, both mentally and physiologically. [15] Many of us can relate to an overload of thoughts just before we want to drift off into sleep. Meditation can bring awareness and relaxation to these stressful thoughts, calming the nervous system and inducing inner peace. How can we apply this knowledge and use meditation as a natural sleep aid?

If you experience sleeping problems, it can be very helpful to meditate every day before going to bed. It is advised to use meditations that calm the mind, for example, focusing on the breath or a candle flame as the object of meditation. You can also do a body scan once you are lying in bed and are ready to drift off into sleep. One effective technique to improve sleep quality is yoga nidra. It is known as a yogic sleep meditation, as it can induce a sleep-like state. Yoga nidra connects us to different levels of consciousness and induces alpha brain wave activity, which is related to relaxation. It activates the parasympathetic nervous system, calming the body and stopping the "fight or flight" response. Stress hormones decrease, and a profound calmness and inner peace can occur. The practice involves focusing on the breath, scanning the body, and expanding the boundaries of the physical body. Practitioners reach a state of deeply relaxed, blissful awareness as they journey through different stages. [16]

Stage 1 – Preparation. Yoga nidra is practiced lying down. Find a comfortable lying position and make sure to keep the body warm and relaxed.

Stage 2 – Initial Relaxation. The practice begins with a body scan. While the body remains motionless, you scan the entire body from head to toe, releasing any tension and bringing relaxation to all parts of the body. This stage usually takes around 10-15 minutes.

Stage 3 – Sankalpa. *Sankalpa* refers to a mental affirmation or mantra, which is repeated and helps us to make positive changes in our lives. Examples include "I am kind," "I am peaceful," "I am accepting of my feelings," and "I fall asleep easily and have a restful, rejuvenating sleep."

Stage 4 – Bodily Visualization. Each part of the body is visualized, and in this way, you become aware of the entire body.

Stage 5 – Awareness of the Breath. Become aware of your breath by focusing on the up and down movements of your abdomen. Start counting these up and down movements from 27 to 0. If you lose count, just start over again.

Stage 6 – Feelings and Sensations. At this stage, different feelings and sensations are evoked by the means of opposites, for example, heavy and light, hot and cold. Focus on these different sensations in your body. This harmonizes the brain hemispheres and releases tension.

Stage 7 – Visualization. Different images are visualized, such as the ocean, the sky, or a forest. This relaxes the mind and promotes inner peace and tranquility.

Stage 8- Sankalpa. At this stage, repeat your positive mental affirmation, three times.

Stage 9 – Externalization. Slowly, bring your awareness back to the physical body. Take your time, and once you feel ready, start moving the body gradually.

You can journey through these stages yourself, or, especially at the beginning, you can use a guided meditation. There are many free, beautiful Yoga Nidra meditations available on the InsightTimer app. Take your time to find a meditation that resonates with you.

HOW I OVERCAME INSOMNIA WITH MEDITATION

When I wake up at, what I like to call "the magic hour" of 2:00 a.m. or something near there, the "what ifs" like to crawl in my ear and cause havoc; everything seems worse at night. Our to-do lists, the problem at work, what so and so said that got back to you... whatever it is, it's just worse. What I like to do when this happens is to go into mantra. *Mantra* is a Sanskrit word that translates to "mind-vehicle". It gives your mind something to do and keeps you away from the ever-so-treacherous rabbit holes. They can even help lift you out of them and bring you back to the present moment. I use a different mantra for "the magic hour" than I use for my morning or afternoon meditations. One that brings me a lot of peace in the wee hours of the morning is an ancient Hawaiian mantra of *Ho'oponopono*. This translates to, "I'm sorry. Please forgive me. Thank you. I love you." It's the ultimate form of reconciliation and forgiveness no matter whose fault- even if one feels justified for harboring negative emotions. I start by taking some very intentional and quiet breaths, to not wake up my husband. This is called ninja breath as you breathe in as quietly and deeply as you can before releasing as quietly and fully as possible. Then silently, to myself, I start repeating the mantra over and over again. When I get distracted by thoughts, sounds, or physical sensations, I come back to my breath and back to my mantra easily and effortlessly. Depending on what is bothering me, the duration of the practice varies. There have been times when it seems like moments and I'm drifting back to sleep. Other times, there are a lot of distractions, i.e., rabbit holes, and it takes me a bit to get present and then drift back into sleep. To be honest, I do not know how I ever drifted to sleep without a mantra. Another mantra to use is, "All is well" or "This too shall pass."

EVENING MEDITATION RITUALS

PREPARING THE MIND FOR SLEEP

Before you sit down for your evening meditation or go to bed, there is a lot you can do to create a beautiful, calming evening that promotes peaceful, high-quality sleep. A typical evening ritual in our household is to lower the volume of anything we are listening to or watching. A cup of hot herbal tea year-round, then we let our dogs out around 8 pm for the final pre-bed potty time. I diffuse lavender essential oil, and we read for a few minutes and sometimes up to an hour before turning out the lights and turning on calming sounds. We have a dedicated speaker in our room just to turn on calming sounds. They run for about an hour before turning off. Taking the time and care to engage in a proper sleep routine can do wonders for your life and is a meditative and intentional practice. Try falling asleep in different ways - to a guided body scan, yoga nidra meditation, or calming sounds and see which practice works best for you. Just remember that trying to go to bed straight from chaos will not often yield results. Be mindful of the hour before you want to be asleep. Turning off digital stimulation an hour before bed, having a bedtime ritual of tea, a shower, calming music, and reading. Engaging the circadian rhythm with a nice dark room keeps the night-time lights dimmer. Experiment and find an evening routine that works best for you. You are invited to immediately put this wisdom into practice – why don't you start tonight by creating your own loving and intentional evening ritual?

GUIDED SLEEP MEDITATIONS

Besides the profound but lengthy practice of yoga nidra, many different meditation practices can help you fall asleep. Body scans work well for falling asleep, along with progressive muscle relaxation. [17] You can either perform the meditation for yourself, and guide yourself through it, or you can listen to a guided meditation. The nice thing about using a guided sleep meditation is that you can just surrender and give in to the meditation and fall asleep. For something as important as falling asleep, my suggestion would be to use a meditation app like Insight Timer as opposed to a free meditation on YouTube. The reason being, no commercials or interruptions and it just goes quiet when it's complete.

Another meditation practice is listening to calming nature sounds such as ocean waves, whale songs, rain, a crackling fire, or crickets. You can use a meditation app for this as well. If you sleep with pets, test the sounds to be sure they approve. I have one dog that does not like rain, thunder, or wind. Just the sound of rain makes her anxious, which then keeps us awake. While you are listening to the sounds, keep your breath slow and steady. When we take long slow deep breaths in and out it sends a signal to our brain that we are safe.

You can also try practicing visualization. Visualize a peaceful scene in which you can deeply relax. Let your worrying thoughts pass by as clouds in the sky or as leaves floating in the river. Deepen your breath and allow your whole body to relax.

No matter what technique you choose, it is very powerful to incorporate gratitude into your meditation. Just being thankful for the day and evoking three things you are grateful for, can shift you into a profound peace and connect you to Source. There is a practice known as the "gratitude rock". For this, you pick any stone or small rock that you like and place it next to your bed. Every evening, just before falling asleep, you place this rock in your hand, hold it tight, and evoke the best thing that happened during your day in gratitude. Drifting off into sleep in a grateful state can create miracles in your life!

THE EFFECTIVENESS OF EVENING MEDITATION

One of my students, Laura, approached me as she was suffering from sleeping problems. At her university, there was an exam period that lasted for four continuous weeks and included a lot of examination and preparation. It seemed impossible for her to have a peaceful sleep; either she couldn't sleep at all, lying awake most of the night, or she would keep waking up during the night. Either way, she felt exhausted during the day and was afraid that the sleeping problem would lower her performance in the examinations. In our conversation, we found that she was studying up to 10 minutes before going to bed, often taking the study material into her bed. We started by separating her room into a sleeping and a study area; no study materials were moved from her study desk, and certainly not brought into the bed. I then suggested to Laura to stop studying at least an hour before bed, although it was difficult for her as she felt the constant pressure to study. Eventually, she managed to free up an hour before bedtime. She would turn off the lights and put candles on, creating a calming, beautiful atmosphere. She would then take the time to do something she enjoys but usually doesn't do during exam periods, like drinking a cup of tea without any distractions or reading her favorite book. Just before sleep, she puts on calming ocean sounds and does a body scan meditation. After just a week of doing this, Laura noticed a significant difference not just in her sleep but also in her general mood and her ability to do well on the exams. She felt that by prioritizing her well-being, she improved the quality of her life immensely.

WAKING UP REFRESHED

MORNING MANTRA MEDITATION PRACTICES

As I mentioned before, having a space to go to for your meditation and doing it first thing, or as close to first things as possible, is going to be the easiest way to cultivate a meditation practice. (Remember what my teacher shared: Rise. Pee. Meditate). As you might notice, the biggest barrier to a consistent meditation practice is the mind chatter. "Today is not a good day".

"Tomorrow, I can meditate again.", "Today I feel too tired." You will see, if you listen to the mind chatter and give in once, chances are you will give in again and again – and gone is your daily meditation practice! Having a firm commitment to meditate first thing in the morning, no matter what, will help cut through all the unproductive and distracting mind chatter.

An easy vehicle for morning meditation are sanskrit mantras. [18] Short phrases are said over and over to connect to the vibration. The vibration is more important than the actual meaning. As humans, we try to put too much meaning into everything we do. The vibration and sound of the mantra are already there and to chant it repeatedly silently without connecting to the meaning helps us to disconnect and enter the gap. Remember the gap? Not the clothing store, but the space in between our thoughts where we are fully in the present moment. Some mantras to begin with are: [19]

"Om Moksha Ritam" = I am emotionally free.

"Lokah Samastah Sukino Bhavantu" = May all beings everywhere be happy and free.

"Om Shanti Shanti Shanti" = Om Peace Peace Peace.

"Sohum" = I am that.

You can start with 5 – 10 minutes. I often share with people to just start with 8 minutes. Set a timer with a peaceful sound to let you know when the 8 minutes are up. Afterward, do not jump into your day right away. Give yourself a few minutes to peacefully breathe and sit in stillness and silence for just a few moments.

MINDFUL START TO THE DAY

Many people check their texts, social media, or email first thing in the morning. I challenge you to start your day mindfully with a routine and to not check anything digital for at least the first 60 minutes of the day. As we discussed in a previous chapter, today's modern technology is highly addictive. This "one short glance" into our emails when waking up likely turns into minutes and then hours. Like the evening ritual, a mindful morning ritual is your opportunity to create a foundation of relaxation and peace in your life. It's a chance to create the conditions for a joyful, successful day. Let's discover a few of the building blocks for a mindful morning so you can choose what works for you and create your personal routine: [20]

Meditation: As we know by now, meditation is the basis for a morning routine (and life). *Rise – Pee – Meditate.*

Journaling: You can journal on how you are feeling, what you are grateful for, or what your intentions are for the day.

Gratitude: Whether it's written, said out loud, or expressed in movement, gratitude is a powerful way to start the day.

Move your body: Whether it's a gentle stretch, yoga, dance, intuitive movement, or a walk in the park – tending to the body has a lot of benefits.

Self-love: Commit to spending 20 minutes doing something you love. Often, our days are so busy that we can't find time for self-care. Make it a priority to integrate self-care into your morning routine. Only when we are feeling well we can live to our highest potential and give to others.

Healthy breakfast: Prepare a healthy, delicious breakfast for yourself and eat mindfully, enjoying every bite.

A quick comment on routines: Our modern days are full of things we feel obliged to do, although we might not enjoy them. The invitation with both the morning and evening routine is to enjoy them – create rituals that bring joy and a sense of wonderment into your life. If you ever find yourself in a routine that feels monotonous or not enjoyable, change things up. The whole purpose is to bring love and lightness into your life, not to add to your endless "to-do" list.

TRANSFORMATION THROUGH ADOPTING A MORNING MEDITATION ROUTINE

My husband and I met in 2015, but he was not a meditator. Obviously, I did not hold it against him, or he would not be my husband today. But after we had been together for a while, I noticed what a hard time he had handling stress and unexpected situations. It was zero to 100. With some encouragement, he started meditating and developed a morning ritual. Over the years, he has become a consistent meditator and has fully adopted a healthy practice. He gets out of bed earlier to accommodate his practice and now handles unexpected situations with more grace and ease. Like anyone, it is a practice. We are always learning, growing, and going deeper within our practice. He stays off his phone and participates in R.P.M. (rise. pee. meditate.) He lights a candle, uses his mala beads, and either does a guided meditation or practices Om Moksha Ritam. Afterward, depending on the weather, he takes one of our dogs on a walk and then does some weight training. It starts his day off on the right track. A solid morning ritual is just as important as an evening ritual. Putting our personal needs first before the day fills in helps us to show up and engage with the best version of ourselves.

Many people ask me, "Can I meditate at 5 pm when I get home from work?" The short answer. Yes. The long answer. There are a million and one things that can get in the way of meditating at 5 pm. The afternoon is a great time for a short afternoon meditation to bring yourself center and present again but putting off your main meditation until 5 pm will almost certainly create a situation of non-priority.

CHAPTER EIGHT
UNLOCKING SELF-AWARENESS THROUGH MEDITATION

Can meditation help individual people overcome limiting beliefs and behaviors that hinder self-growth and self-discovery? From my personal experience, the answer is yes. Do you have rigid or limiting beliefs? We have all grown up in conditioning, one way or another. We inherit limiting beliefs from our parents or caregivers, religious leaders, teachers, and surroundings. I grew up in a very conservative area in Utah, and I was not part of the culture. However, I had limiting beliefs from just growing up in the culture. Rigid beliefs can span anything from being inflexible in your personal lives to condemning others for not believing the same thing. Meditation helps you to identify what is no longer serving you on a deeper level. It helps you to pull back the many layers of conditioning and become a better version of yourself.

THE JOURNEY WITHIN

SELF-REFLECTION AND MEDITATION

Self-reflection can be a positive practice when done right. It's not about going back in time and feeling justified in an action or emotion or fantasizing about what you would like to have said to that person. Rather, it's a practice to create a distance from the emotion, thought, or action and to observe it from a more neutral perspective. Usually, we are "in it". We are so absorbed in whatever circumstance it is that we dramatize and think about it over and over again. We bring the past into the present. And no judgment - this is just the nature of the human mind. With meditation, however, we can leap from being caught in a situation towards reflection, reconciliation, forgiveness, and love. We can see the situation or person through the eyes of love rather than through the eyes of our ego with all its filters. We can find compassion for ourselves and others. Finally, often, after many years, we can put something to rest with love so we can move on. In essence, self-reflection is a process of becoming more self-aware. We reconnect to our inner selves and start seeing all the thoughts, emotions, and stories for what they are.[1] This perspective of being the witness is a way to explore whether life situations still align with us, to see where we need to move on and to understand where we are still learning. Staying anchored in self-compassion is the key to self-reflection, as, at times, it might be uncomfortable to reflect on certain aspects of our lives. This is not an opportunity to judge ourselves but to lovingly witness the stories we tell ourselves.

To practice self-reflection, start your meditation as usual by focusing on an object such as the breath. Once you feel ready, you can start asking yourself open-ended questions such as "Am I truly happy?", "What pattern keeps recurring in my life?" or "How can I become more of my true self?" [2] You can ask any questions that are loving and relevant to you. Try not to overanalyze the answers, but receive whatever comes up with love and compassion. You might want to write your answers in a journal. Observe any patterns or thoughts that are not serving you any longer and that don't express who you truly are. See if there is anything you would like to forgive yourself and others. Find opportunities to bring more love into your life. Once you feel complete, conclude the self-reflection with a Metta practice.

RECOGNIZING PATTERNS

Research has shown that most people spend about 47% of their day in a state of "autopilot," meaning they act automatically, lost in the realm of thoughts, without awareness of the present moment.[3] We unconsciously repeat the same thoughts, emotions, and habits every day and wonder why our life never changes. These patterns are mostly the result of programming we received from our environment when we grew up. Children between the ages of 2 and 6 are in a state of neurological development and operate on a *theta* brain wave frequency, which is a state in which the brain is very suggestible to programming.[4] The programs we receive are installed into our subconscious mind, just like software is installed on a computer, regardless of whether we like the programs or not. They run in the background, guide our thoughts and actions, and usually become deeply ingrained into our identity and more unconscious and subtle as time goes by. [5] This means as we go through life, we are run by programs we didn't even consciously choose, rather than being guided by our most authentic selves. Is this simply the predicament of living in this modern world with all the distractions, technology, and pressure to just go through our days, from task to task, without a deeper awareness of ourselves? Only if this is what we choose there is a way to break out of this cycle. And this way is the practice of meditation. Meditation is a tool to become aware of the programs that automatically run us, to break out of these patterns, and to live a more conscious life that expresses who we really are, in our essence.[6] Let's discover the roadmap through which meditation helps us to break the cycle of living on autopilot.

1. TRANSCENDING THE MIND CHATTER

Meditation, firstly, helps us to go beyond our habitual thoughts and stories by bringing us back to an awareness of pure consciousness, which lies beyond all the chatter of the mind. There is a distance between us, as awareness, thoughts, and emotions. This means that limiting programs stop controlling us as we become more conscious of them.[7] You start to become aware of patterns that keep playing out in your life: Attracting unavailable partners, money problems, health conditions, and stagnancy in your career are all examples of subconscious loops playing themselves out.

2. TAKING RESPONSIBILITY FOR YOUR LIFE

As you start becoming aware of the patterns in your life, it is essential to take responsibility for them. Although you start to understand that childhood conditioning led you into these situations, it is up to you whether you stay stuck or break out of them. If we go a step further, often there are certain lessons for us to learn from these situations. Once we understand this and learn a lesson, the undesirable situation in our lives often disappears, and we grow into a more authentic version of ourselves.[8] Thus, we adopt the mindset that everything happens for us to grow and evolve.

3. ENTERING PURE CONSCIOUSNESS

As the mind becomes quieter and meditation deepens, we start to access pure consciousness. This consciousness is to be experienced in the gaps between thoughts. It is the witness consciousness, and as we deepen into it, we start to realize that the same witness consciousness is present in everyone. It is like the light of consciousness shining through us and with that, illuminating the light of every other being. We start seeing all the programs for what they are: simply programs on top of our true essence; they are not who we really are.

4. PURIFYING THE PATTERNS

As we enter deeper states of consciousness, the mind is automatically purified. Our subconscious patterns, called *samskaras* in traditional texts on meditation, can't withstand the illuminating light and power of pure consciousness; they are consumed by higher states of consciousness. In the philosophy of meditation, this transformational state is described as *Nirodha parinama,* the mental transformation of dissolution. As we rest in the gap for prolonged periods, thoughts cease, our *samskaras* dissolve, and our consciousness is permeated by pure existence and presence. [9] This is a process that happens automatically as we rest in deep presence; it can't be understood by the mind. It is what happens when we stay in the gap.

5. BREAKING THE CYCLE

As we engage in this deep, transformational work in our meditation practice, we will inevitably notice changes in our lives. However, it is important to also bring the insights consciously from meditation into your daily life. This means to choose to be aware as patterns occur and to set the intention to change them. In his book "Breaking the Habit of Being Yourself," Dr. Joe Dispenza describes a powerful method to change our patterns. In short, once you become aware of a limiting thought or pattern, you interfere by saying "change," creating a gap or a moment of awareness, and then you create a more empowering thought. For example, there might be a thought repeating itself unconsciously, such as "I'm only attracting unavailable men, no matter what I do." You see the thought, pause, and realize that it's much more empowering to think, "I have the power to attract an available and loving partner into my life." Then, you go even deeper and look at the situation in your life that reflects this thought and how you keep perpetuating it. Once you find the lesson, you see it clearly and something shifts. You don't perpetuate the pattern anymore, and you start attracting different situations into your life. Or, in the example, different men. Whether we want it or not, our patterns repeat themselves in the same situations, just in different expressions or people, until we see it and transform it. As Pema Chodron said: *"Nothing ever goes away until it teaches us what we need to know."*

SELF-DISCOVERY THROUGH MEDITATION

Our patterns can be so subtle that we do not even see them. A pattern I had to break free from was inviting narcissistic and over-controlling partners into my life. I have a strong personality. I'm very independent, and I never thought this would be a problem. But the truth is, it was a pattern from childhood that I could not see. It was comfortable, and I was accustomed to the feeling until one day, something shifted. I saw it. I knew I needed help to define it. Help to figure out what to do and help to move on. It did not stop there, as the universe brought me another narcissistic partner in different packaging, and another... and another until I said, enough! Through meditation and the power of cultivating a solid practice, it revealed who I really was. I no longer needed the attention of someone who only wanted my adoration for self-serving purposes. I no longer had the desire to be the people pleaser... to be the glue holding everything together. The lesson had been taught, and shortly after, a more authentic partner entered my life.

MINDFULNESS IN RELATIONSHIPS

COMMUNICATION AND EMPATHY

Communication and empathy, and I'll take it even further to compassion, are at the forefront of every healthy relationship. Empathy describes the ability to understand and share the feelings of another. Compassion means a concern for the sufferings or misfortunes of others and to take action to relieve that suffering. Basically, compassion is not so much about pity but more about sharing the suffering of another. As Stephen Levine said: *"When your fear touches someone's pain, it becomes pity; when your love touches someone's pain, it becomes compassion."* Pity is an energizing of our ego, whereas compassion dissolves the ego.

Eventually, in every relationship, conflicts can develop, and it's important to have a basis of compassion and understanding from which conflicts can be looked at and brought back into harmony. Meditation can bring about feelings to process, gain clarity on a situation, and grow gratitude and compassion together. Having a meditation practice can help couples to create positive coping mechanisms and strategies. Research has found that mindfulness is an important predictor of relationship quality and conflict resolution. Acting with awareness seems to be an important factor to enhance the quality of a relationship. Mindfulness-based relationship enhancement (MBRE) helps couples to prevent and peacefully resolve conflicts by enhancing communication and empathy.[10] The building blocks of MBRE are mindfulness, acceptance, relaxation, and self-broadening.[11] Mindfulness means to be rooted in the present moment, in non-judgment, and to create a gap between the situation and our reaction. Acceptance allows both partners to accept the situation as it is, understanding both did the best they could with their level of consciousness at the time and develop compassion and empathy for themselves and their partner. Relaxation prevents an immediate reaction out of tension and can enhance well-being, clarity, and calmness. Self-broadening describes the process of broadening our sense of self to include other beings. An additional important component of MBRE is to gain more insight into our patterns and how they play out in the relationship. MBRE has been shown to increase relationship satisfaction, closeness, and acceptance of the partner and to lower distress in relationships.[12]

RESOLVING CONFLICTS

How can we resolve conflicts in relationships once they arise? Based on MBRE, there are several ways to restore harmony. Before you start any conversation to resolve a conflict, it is suggested to disconnect from the outside world, for example by putting your phone away, to be completely present with your partner. You can meditate together or practice eye gazing to deepen your awareness. From this space of connectedness, you can then listen actively to what your partner is sharing – don't think about what you want to say, don't judge their perspective, just listen with open attention. You can stay curious and ask questions to understand them better. Rather than reacting emotionally to what your partner shared, you can respond by first taking a break, tending to any emotions you might have, and then responding with clarity and love. Try seeing your partner through new eyes, through the eyes of love, rather than through filters and judgments. When the conflict is resolved, you can express acknowledgment and gratitude towards your partner, create a vision for your relationship together and embrace each other. You can also incorporate mindful touch into your everyday life.

Another powerful practice to resolve conflicts is Metta meditation, unconditional loving kindness. It helps to elevate our own emotions and see others for their humanness. Knowing that everyone is doing their best, from where they are in life, in that current moment. Including ourselves. We need to turn the Metta towards ourselves and our partners. Have you ever done something and afterward thought, "I feel like a jerk!"? I know I have. Then you beat yourself up. Then you do it again, and again, and again until self-loathing starts to settle in around a particular situation. Or, your partner does something, and every time you have the chance to bring it back up, you do. You let them know how wrong it was and what a jerk move it was. When at the end of the day, in order to heal and move past it, what you really need is unconditional loving kindness to grow some compassion and to recognize that we are where we are. We learn, and then we do better. This is not meant to frost over abuse. Abuse needs to be remedied, and if you are in a situation with abuse, the Metta needs to be turned to yourself first and foremost. Ask for help from someone other than your abuser. Later on, after things settle, you can practice Metta and forgiveness far away, from a safe distance.

HOW MEDITATION TRANSFORMED A STRAINED RELATIONSHIP

One of my students, Natalie, shared with me that she was about to break up with her partner of 7 years because the relationship was full of conflict. Even though they knew how to live together in peace, for the last year, the disharmony has been stronger than the peacefulness. We discovered that despite knowing each other very well, both partners stopped communicating openly and acknowledging each other. Rather, they kept complaining, seeing faults, and were caught in a cycle of negative thinking. After learning about the importance of mindfulness, Natalie decided to introduce three elements of mindful relationships into the connection with her partner: Disconnecting from the outside world, active listening, and eye gazing. They made it a ritual to sit together for 30 minutes at the end of each day, disconnecting from everything apart from each other, eye gazing for a few minutes, and then sharing and actively listening. Natalie found that the combination of being fully present with each other and sharing openly was very healing for the relationship, as finally, both were able to see and acknowledge each other again and to see each other through the eyes of love.

My last update was that Natalie and her partner got married and restored the harmony in their relationship.

EMBRACING CHANGE AND GROWTH

LETTING GO OF THE PAST

Yesterday is gone and if you are ruminating on it, it is robbing you of the present. Many situations have caused us heartache or stress, and we haven't fully processed it, which is why similar situations keep coming back up again and again. Letting go of the past so you can be fully present is a gift. In this process, you must ask yourself if you are being a victim, not accepting responsibility for the part you play. Are you projecting your pain onto others? Is your ego running down the street shouting the justification to everyone within earshot? There are three sides to every story, their side, your side, and the truth. Observing the situation from an outside perspective while releasing the drama and emotional charge can help you lay it to rest. And here is the tricky part: Our ego loves drama. If we experience an unwanted situation over and over again, chances are that a hidden part of us gets some gratification from it. It keeps our ego alive and resists when we try to release the emotional charge of the situation. In practice, how can we overcome these barriers? Let go of the past and start to truly live in the now.[13]

1. FEEL THE EMOTIONS

Whatever emotions there are about the situation from your past, allow yourself to feel them. These emotions keep you stuck in the loop. Feeling them and releasing the energetic charge sets you free. It is often said: "Feeling is healing."

2. SEE THE SITUATION FROM THEIR PERSPECTIVE

Remember that everyone is doing their best, with the level of consciousness they are at. If another person was involved in the situation, try to understand their perspective and reasons for acting the way they did. This doesn't mean to agree with them, but you open yourself to a new perspective.

3. TAKE RESPONSIBILITY

We all make mistakes and end up in undesired situations. That's part of life. It's essential however to take responsibility for our life. Only when we take responsibility, can we change a situation. Outsourcing responsibility to others means we wait for other people to correct the situation when most likely they are not able to, as this is our task.

4. BE IN THE NOW

Actively focus on being present in the moment. All our problems come from thinking excessively about the past or the future. Do whatever helps you to stay present: meditate, go for a walk in nature, practice gratitude, engage in self-care, or cook your favorite meal while staying present. Accepting everything can seem difficult, but it's an important part of living in the now and letting go of the past. Whatever the current circumstance may be, you can learn from it and use it to create a better future, or you can stay stuck, letting the circumstances control you.

5. MEDITATE

Sometimes, when a situation seems to have a strong hold on you, or the same negative story keeps repeating itself, the best thing you can do is to sit down and focus all your attention on an object of meditation. Set a timer for 5 minutes and stay aware of your breath. This naturally quiets the mind, and even after just a few minutes, the situation doesn't seem as overwhelming anymore.

SETTING INTENTIONS

A beautiful practice is to set intentions just for the day, the week, or an outcome you would like to see unfold. It helps you to see that you are the common denominator in your life events and that things don't just happen randomly. Your intention is something that resonates with your very being, it feels good. It lays out a clear path towards taking deliberate action.[14] It's sending a signal to the universe about what it is you would like to call into your life. The most powerful way to set an intention is to meditate on it, to first get clear about what outcome you would like to create for yourself. Then, write it down, in your journal or a piece of paper that you see often during your day. As you go through your day, do your best to stay aligned with your intention. If any resistance or difficulty arises, do the necessary inner work to stay on track with your desired outcome.[15]

PERSONAL GROWTH ACHIEVED THROUGH MEDITATION

Before I started a consistent meditation practice, my livelihood always seemed to be so dependent on circumstance. At one time when I was younger, I worked four different jobs to make ends meet. I could have chosen to work at a local factory, which I did for a while, but factory life was not for me. It just always seemed that I was a day late and a dollar short. It was the pay, it was the hours, it was the small town I lived in. My boss did not like me; they did not see my worth. Whatever it was, the excuse was all the same. I moved to a different state and found work that took care of the bills with a few dollars extra. Then I joined direct sales and had a good run for about five years. I worked hard, built a business, and a team... and then the company closed their at-home division. I opened a boutique, the economy crashed, and all these things just kept happening to me. By this time, I was a single mama and needed to make sure I took care of business. My meditation was becoming more consistent about this time but it wasn't perfect. Opportunities would come, I would take them... because they were good, but they would end. All sorts of reasons: company closing, the company sold, the boss was in a different dimension. A funny thing happened: the more consistent my meditation became, the more consistent my livelihood became. Slowly, gradually, and subtly my life started shifting as I was growing and becoming a better version of myself. I finally landed a great job and stayed for four years and would be there today if I had not moved and started my own business. Now, I have run my own business for longer than I have been at any one job. It takes care of me and my family, and we can go on vacations, manage our own time, and have freedoms we would not have had before. Being consistent in my practice, letting go of limiting beliefs, breaking down the layers of conditioning, and growing compassion and gratitude have all contributed to my success.

CHAPTER NINE
MEDITATION FOR EMOTIONAL RESILIENCE

"When we surrender, we allow the universe to work its magic; we say yes to infinite possibilities; we trust that things will work out as they are meant to; and we give ourselves permission to let go of the outcome. This can be liberating, intimidating, blissful, scary, and a swirl of so many other emotions. But in the end, if we are true to our heart, life unfolds with magnificence... and we get to celebrate"

— *davidji*

Resilience is the ability to overcome a difficult situation and get back to the pre-difficult state of being. There is not much we can control in life. We can control how we show up, how we engage, and how we react. The sooner we surrender to this and allow the universe to do its thing, the sooner we can get back to our peaceful state of being.

COPING WITH LIFE'S CHALLENGES

MEDITATION AS EMOTIONAL ARMOR

Wait... don't we want to melt away emotional armor? Yes, we do when it comes to defensiveness, trauma, rigidity, or an overactive ego that thinks everybody and everything is out to get us. But having meditative emotional armor is a little bit different. Being able to control our emotions to be less reactive allows us to see situations and people with more clarity. When this happens, we can make better decisions. It also helps us to understand that we have no idea what someone else is going through at any given time. Not one person we engage with during any given day wakes up saying, "Boy, I am really out to get Jane today! I'm going to make her life miserable. Now, where is she?" Movies and social media may make us think otherwise. But the reality is the world does not revolve around how we feel, and taking things personally does not do us one bit of good. In fact, the world is not out to get us. It's not for us either. It just is. When we enter the day with this state of mind, very little rattles our cage. When someone cuts us off in traffic, instead of being mad at them we are grateful we had our eyes on the road, and no one was hurt. We see things from an entirely different perspective. We see things from a place of compassion and acceptance rather than from our trauma and defensiveness.

Having a meditative emotional armor can help us with anxious and fearful thoughts we encounter in daily life. For example, daily, we might be thinking: "What if I'm stuck in traffic and I'm late for work again? My boss will fire me." We go down a rabbit hole of thoughts and stories, and the body becomes tense. The "fight or flight" response is activated. With a consistent meditation practice, we start identifying such thoughts and can reframe them. From a clearer and more accepting perspective, we can ask ourselves: "What are the odds of me losing my job because I'm stuck in a traffic jam this morning?" And, considering a highly unlikely outcome, we can inquire: "If the worst-case scenario happens, is it true that I have strategies to cope with it? Didn't I want to look for a new and more exciting job anyway? Can I trust that the Universe has my back?" [1] With that, our meditative amor releases the fearful energy behind daily negative thoughts.

TECHNIQUES FOR RESILIENCE

We can't deny that sometimes, life takes us by surprise. An adversity presents itself – someone we know passes away, we unexpectedly lose our job, are diagnosed with an illness, or our partner suddenly declares they want to end our relationship. Developing the ability to move through such crises healthily is referred to as resilience.[2] Dedicating effort to developing resilience means we can deal better with adversity and recover more quickly. This doesn't mean there is no pain; rather, we know how to deal with emotional pain in a more constructive, loving way.

Practices to increase our resilience include self-care practices such as finding time to relax, spending time in nature, and looking after our physical body.[3] It can also be very helpful to have a strong support network of friends or family with whom we can share how we truly feel.

An important, more practical strategy for resilience is to change the narrative of a situation. Usually, we ruminate on the challenging event; we evoke it in our minds again and again, staying stuck in a cycle of overthinking. After we allow the pain of a situation to arise and process it, we can consciously change how we speak and think about the event. You can evoke the challenging event and come up with three positive things about it. We start focusing on the bright side. It certainly doesn't mean that suddenly everything is "love and light" – but it means we choose a more empowering perspective. We don't create an insurmountable problem out of the situation.[4] And whom does it serve anyway when we keep ruminating over a past event for weeks, months, or even years?

Changing the narrative is a practice that can be easily implemented into everyday life. In this case, you change any words you speak to more positive words. What the lips say, the ears hear, and the mind believes. Speak things out loud, be grateful, and express gratitude. "She is just way too grateful in life." - has anyone ever muttered those words? After that person pulls out in front of you, say out loud, "Wow, I hope they get to where they need to be safely. It must be important." Instead of shaking your fist or flipping the bird, send them words of love and blessings. My friend Paulette made something called a "Blessing Rod" for this very thing. The first time we used it we were on a 1000-mile road trip and had so much fun sending blessings to everyone that we perceived ourselves as not being optimal drivers. We laughed with love and people wondered what in the world we were doing.

Paulette Esposito is a Messenger, Intuitive Counselor, Psychic Medium, Coach and Ordained Interfaith Minister. The Blessing Rod was a message she received many years ago. Today the Blessing Rod message, "I Bless you and Send you into the Light of Love," is needed more than ever. Go to BlessingRod.com and learn how to use it to change lives, including your own, and to contact Paulette for more information. Together, we can create PEACE and spread LOVE every day.

TRIUMPH OVER ADVERSITY THROUGH MEDITATION

One of my students, Paula, recently shared a story with me. She was a single mom and suddenly lost her job. She didn't have much savings with rent, and bills to pay and a little girl to look after. Her thoughts were racing, and she was constantly in survival mode. The only moments of peace were during her daily 15-minute morning meditation. Rather than just focusing on her breath, as she usually did, she started working with this challenging situation during her meditation. She would allow herself to feel the fear, the frustration, and the shame and to release the energetic charge behind these emotions. She also started to observe her negative thoughts about the situation and realized how she was constantly telling herself she might be homeless soon. Instead, she started telling herself that she has the inner resources and resilience to find a new job that pays her even better and gives her more time with her daughter. She started to express gratitude for this situation, allowing her to reinvent herself. Paula started to trust that, in the end, everything would work out. It didn't take her long to find a new job that indeed paid her better. She also started her own photography business on the side, which, after a while became her full-time job which allowed her to manage her own time and spend as much time with her daughter as she liked.

HANDLING GRIEF AND LOSS

THE ROLE OF MEDITATION IN HEALING

There is a story of a monk who, when he arrived in the US, had severe health problems. His right leg had developed gangrene, a dangerous condition in which the blood flow to a body part is cut off.[5] The monk was hospitalized and examined by three different doctors in New York City, all of whom said that the leg needed to be amputated. The monk consulted the Dalai Lama, who advised not to amputate the leg, and to engage in meditative healing practices.[6] The monk took a leap of faith, engaged in intensive healing meditations and after one year, the leg was healed. This is a stunning example of faith-based healing and the power of the mind.

In today's world, we are very aware of the connection between our mind and the physical body. We keep hearing about the increasing occurrence of psychosomatic disorders - conditions in which our mind and psychological stress adversely affect our body's health. Psychosomatic conditions include hypertension, respiratory illness, gastrointestinal symptoms, migraine, impotence, and many more.[7] It is no surprise that our body becomes affected by the stress our mind creates – as we discovered earlier, the average person perceives so many stressors in their daily life, that the "fight or flight response" is continuously active. If our mind can create disease, can it also create healing?

These days, science indeed acknowledges that the mind is a powerful healing tool. When the mind heals, emotions can heal, and the body can heal. Researchers are speaking about the "placebo effect", which describes the healing of a person's physical or mental health condition after receiving a placebo treatment, rather than an actual treatment.[8] Thus, the health benefit can't be attributed to a medicine and occurs due to a person's thoughts and beliefs. In his book "You Are the Placebo", Dr. Joe Dispenza shares that through meditation, people can heal even from diseases that are labeled as incurable, by using the power of their minds. He describes a meditative process by which an individual first disconnects from their current environment and personality and enters into altered brain states in which neural connections are changed, and a new, healthy person is created. And the fascinating fact is that it works! There are hundreds of case studies, including medical reports and brain scans, which show that meditation alters the brain and leads to healing.[9]

MEDITATIVE PRACTICES FOR GRIEF

Loss is one of those events that leaves us in deep pain. We experience grief – a strong emotional response after a loss.[10] This can be the loss of a loved one, of a job, a relationship, a pet, or a friend. Grief can affect us on all levels of our being. There are emotional effects as well as physical, for example, poor sleep quality, a decline in cognitive functioning, decreased immunity, and digestive issues.[11]

Meditation can help with our mental health, as we learn to quiet the mind with all its chatter and dramatization of the event. It also helps us to access our emotions, rather than suppressing them. When moving through grief, meditation can also help us to improve our sleep and to relax and heal the body, as the parasympathetic nervous system is activated, and the stress response stops.[12]

Another, more spiritual benefit of meditation to process grief is that it helps us understand the impermanence of life, which is the core of the Buddhist teachings. Life is constantly changing, and yet we resist it. So much of our suffering comes from grasping and attaching ourselves to certain people, situations, and life circumstances. We look for happiness everywhere in the outside world, ignoring the truth that this happiness won't last. The only unchanging aspect in this universe is our pure awareness of being, also called Buddha nature, which is the real source of happiness. Any loss is a painful but powerful reminder of impermanence and reminds us to live in the moment and to deepen our awareness. Many monks meditate deliberately on death, to release any attachments to the world, and to realize their true, unchanging Self.

If this sounds very challenging for you, some gentler practices can help with grief.[13] One powerful practice is to begin your meditation by focusing on an object and to then focus on healing mantras such as:

I give myself permission and time to grieve.
I am safe to feel all my emotions.

My grieving process is unique and has its own timing.
I learn and grow from this experience.
I reach out and ask for help when I need it.
I will be kind and loving to myself through this process.
I know this too shall pass, and I know I'm getting through this.
I am grateful for all the blessings in my life today.

Another practice that can be included in your daily routine when experiencing grief is self-compassion meditation.[14] For this, focus all your attention on embracing yourself and any experience you have in love. Allow yourself to feel anything, and say kind, encouraging words to yourself. Remember that you always did the best you could and that you can move through anything. As Rumi said: *"What hurts you, blesses you. Darkness is your candle."*

HOW MEDITATION HELPS TO NAVIGATE GRIEF

When my father committed suicide, I was shocked beyond belief. True shock, the kind that stops your breath, the kind that makes it impossible to take a breath in. It was like the wind had been knocked out of me and I was lying flat on my back with a ton of bricks on my chest. The grief that came afterward felt unbearable. My life went into turmoil and when it was finally time to heal there was so much to unpack. Grief, anger, why me, sadness, emptiness, and blame. I longed for a father but not one with anger, narcissism, and addiction. I longed for a healthy and loving father. One that would take me places and go out to lunch with me. But by this time, there had been six years of living in the muddy water, and it was time to let the mud settle so I could see clearly again. Meditation practices were my lifesaver. I had practiced on and off throughout my life but in more of a crisis meditator way. I started with a few times a week and then would do walking meditations by myself in the foothills. It was a getaway for me. A place to listen to the birds, the sound of the rocks and dirt under my feet and to feel the elements. All of this started to help me rebuild myself and discover who I was. Eventually, I became a consistent meditator, and it allowed me time to let the mud settle. It allowed me to see that my father did not wake up one day with the thought of ruining his kids and family's lives. He was just doing himself. He was doing the best he could at that moment with what he had been given in life. There is no doubt that if I had been following a consistent practice it would have been a smoother process, still pain and grief, but a smoother recovery.

THRIVING IN UNCERTAIN TIMES

MEDITATION DURING CRISES

As the world as a collective went through the global COVID-19 pandemic a few years ago, we are all aware of how quickly and dramatically a crisis can occur and change our lives. While many people think of meditation as a practice done in a calm, quiet environment, the truth in our modern world is that we can find ourselves in situations that are not peaceful, but rather challenging and often disastrous. Whether it's a global pandemic, a natural disaster like an earthquake, the sudden loss of a loved one, or a traffic accident – not one of us is safe from these occurrences. But keeping up a consistent meditation practice, and building our meditative armor, can help us stay connected to an inner stillness and peacefulness, even during crisis. A friend and fellow meditation teacher shared with me that she was teaching a silent meditation retreat when suddenly the hall started to shake. It was only a light earthquake that lasted a few seconds, but this short moment felt threatening. It was interesting to observe that not a single student panicked. Many of them just kept meditating, some opened their eyes to see what was happening and continued meditating once the shaking stopped.

In any crisis, you will find that there is an initial shock reaction in the body – the "fight or flight" response gets activated. And this time, finally for the reason it evolved – to keep us safe in life-threatening situations. With a consistent meditation practice, there is still this moment of shock, but it happens on a background of stillness. Once you get to know this background in your meditation practice, nothing, no crisis, can completely shake you, as you are anchored in stillness within.

Also, scientific studies found that meditation helps to navigate crises. A study showed that mindfulness meditation reduces anxiety, depression, and physical pain scores, and recommends a meditation practice during crises such as a global pandemic, pandemic, as it is a low-cost method that can relieve anxiety across the population.[15] Scientists emphasize that mindfulness can help with relaxation, and creates a gap between our initial emotions in a crisis, and our response.[16] The more consistent our practice in daily life, the more prepared we are for when a crisis hits us, and the more we can support ourselves and others.

CULTIVATING INNER STRENGTH

People who meditate often see unexpected situations that come up as a challenge rather than a stress point. We release our attachment to a situation, which brings about peace and calmness. This openness helps us to see the situation from an outside perspective rather than someone in the thick of it, allowing us to have more clarity and more courage. At times, we need to be decisive and think quickly. Studies have shown that meditation is associated with beneficial changes in brain areas known for cognitive functioning, emotion regulation, and empathy, and improves decision-making.[17] How can meditation support us to have more clarity, courage, and decision-making skills? It cultivates inner strength in us. Inner strength connects us to our inherent willpower, resilience, courage, and discipline. It leads us to empowered ways of thinking and acting and to create positive changes in the world.[18] It enhances our self-worth, our ability to take aligned action, and our assertiveness. As we meditate, we become more and more aware of our true Self, of awareness, and we awaken our hearts. As we drop from the mind, with all its "I can't," into the heart, our inner strength starts to cultivate and radiate naturally. We connect to our intuition and find back to an inner balance, an openness, from which everything is perceived with more spaciousness.

RESILIENCE THROUGH MEDITATION DURING CHALLENGING CIRCUMSTANCES

One of my students, Beatrice, worked in conflict resolution. She would travel to areas of war and conflict to manage the supply of resources for those in need. Beatrice ended up at the meditation center as she experienced burnout and didn't know what to do. Although she loved her job, she found it increasingly difficult to be confronted with so much suffering and instability in her living situation. She started to have a daily 20-minute meditation practice in which she first focused on an object, and then concluded with a Metta meditation. As she deepened her practice, Beatrice found that she felt much more centered in herself. She started to be more self-aware and observe all the thoughts and emotions about her work from a distance. This helped her process a lot of emotions that were stuck in her body. She would allow herself to feel these emotions, rather than reacting to them. As she started to send blessings to the war zones where she used to work every day, she realized that there are ways to help the people who are suffering, other than traveling to the war zones at the expense of her health. One morning, after meditation, the idea occurred to apply for a promotion, which meant she would be in a managerial position in one of the offices. She was offered the promotion without any barriers and found herself to have so much more productivity as she kept up her daily meditation. The results of consistent practice not only helped her but transformed her and Beatrice knows that meditation is a valuable tool for maintaining resilience and well-being no matter what life throws her way. Meditation has led to greater personal and professional success.

CHAPTER TEN
THE MODERN MEDITATOR'S TOOLKIT

It is estimated that 275 million people meditate around the world.[1] In the US alone, statistics show that around 38 million people practice meditation.[2] About 92% of practitioners meditate to relax and reduce stress, which is no surprise in our modern, fast-paced world.[3] The ancient practice of meditation is finally being applied to change the lives of people in these modern times. At the beginning of our meditation journey, we focus a lot on having consistent practice in the morning. At some point, however, our entire life becomes a meditation. We act more from the present moment, connect with Source, and bring awareness to what we do. Rather than blindly following our thoughts, we become conscious of them and choose what we want to think. All of this is closer to you than you might think, and the way to get there is by incorporating meditation into your daily activities. All you have to do is say yes!

INTEGRATING MEDITATION INTO DAILY LIFE

MINDFUL EVERYDAY ACTIVITIES

Anything you do during your day can be turned into meditation when you do it mindfully. I heard a teacher say that it's not about integrating meditation into our daily life but about integrating daily life into our meditation! That is not to say that mindful practice throughout the day is a substitute for consistent morning practice – but at some point, it becomes one coherent practice. Our entire life becomes a meditation. For the beginning the best way to start is to find "mini-meditation immersions". These brief moments of meditation are easy to create throughout the day. Let's do one right now. Take a deep breath in slow and steady and release just as slow and steady. Take a moment to feel what is supporting you right now. A chair, sofa, the bed... whatever is supporting you. Really feel it and the gravity allowing your body to rest upon it while you read. Now feel your shirt touching your skin and your pants on your legs. Feel the temperature of the room and the space around you. Breathe. You just did it! A mini-meditation moment.[4]

You can also integrate mini meditation moments into every day activities by choosing to do things mindfully. When washing the dishes, notice the soap bubble, watch the water rinse the dishes, and listen to the sound of the water, the sound of the dish settling in the strainer. Doing the dishes with such attention that you are fully in the present moment—the same with eating. Let your eyes feast upon the meal, express gratitude before eating, notice the texture, and the colors, take time to smell the flavors of your meal, and allow your stomach to growl and your mouth to water. As you take bites, feel the texture, and the temperature, and allow your tastebuds time to fully enjoy the flavor profiles of each bite you take. Swallow with intention and allow the food to reach your stomach before taking another bite. Remember to breathe. This is doing everyday practices mindfully.

If you find it difficult to remember those mini-mindful moments in your busy daily life, choose one of your daily activities that will be transformed into meditation. For example, taking your shower in the morning, dressing yourself, or eating breakfast. Deciding on one clear activity acts like an anchor and reminds you every day to engage in this activity as a meditation. Over time, you will find that this mindfulness automatically extends to other daily activities.

TECHNIQUES FOR TRANSFORMING DAILY LIFE INTO MEDITATION

If it still seems challenging for you to integrate meditation into your daily life, don't worry. There are some specific techniques you can use at the beginning. These techniques are very simple and only require one thing: Saying yes to bringing mindfulness into your day.

WALKING MEDITATION

You can integrate meditation every time you are walking somewhere. From the bed to your bathroom. From the car to your office. Going to grab a snack on your lunch break. All of us walk many steps every day, but most of the time without awareness! With walking meditation, we bring awareness to every step. Become aware of the movement of walking – lifting the sole of the foot, moving the foot, and then placing it on the ground. Focus all your attention on the movement. Then, imagine that as you place your foot on the floor, it is touching the floor. As you lift the foot, a white lotus is blossoming. Whenever any thoughts distract you, come back to the movements of your feet. For your first walking meditation, it's advisable to practice in a quiet, calm space, before you can extend it to your everyday walks in daily life.

"I AM AWARE" GAME

The idea of this game is to remember ourselves as awareness to reconnect to the stillness within, during our busy daily lives. Choose any object that you are likely going to use a lot during the day, for example, a pen or a water bottle. Whenever you pick up the object during your day, say silently to

116

yourself or out loud, "I am aware." You can start this practice with seven days and extend it for as long as you like. If you have friends who meditate, you can make this game even more fun by saying, "I am aware," whenever your friend gives you any object that you then touch. You can also remind each other when you forget to say, "I am aware." Bonus tip: You can practice this game with your partner!

THE 5-MINUTE BREATH

Set a reminder for three times a day, for example, for after your morning routine, your lunch break and after dinner. Find times that are convenient and fit into your schedule. Whenever the timer goes off, practice meditation by focusing on your breath for just 5 minutes. You will see what a huge difference this makes in your daily life!

I AM AWARENESS

Find a period during your day of 5 to 20 minutes in which you stay focused on pure awareness of being, the I AM. For instance, during a walk in the park, or when having a meal. Focus all your attention on the words "I AM." You will get distracted at some point, and whenever you notice it, come back to the I AM. Eventually, there will be longer periods in which you just rest in pure awareness.

THE SEAMLESS INTEGRATION OF MEDITATION

My students keep telling me that nature helps them a lot to integrate meditation into their lives. When they go for a walk in the forest, or on the beach, and even out foraging, it's so much easier to feel the connectedness of all things. To see the beauty of a bird, a flower, or a tree and to understand that there is an innate intelligence within all of life, including us humans. When we watch the waves or the trees in the wind, it's so easy to deepen into the present moment. However, as soon as we return to human chaos, these moments can be easily forgotten. One of my students shared with me that she placed "awareness reminders" everywhere in her house. She wrote "present moment" on little pieces of paper and placed them wherever she would see them during her day – her bed, the door, desk, window, and fridge. Whenever she saw one of these reminders, she paused and came back to the present moment. You can also write reminders with the words "awareness," "love," "stillness," or whatever resonates with you. Another student shared how she started to turn every meal into a meditation and that in the end, her whole family joined. Not only did her family benefit from increased mindfulness, but they also noticed a decrease in the usual arguments over the dinner table until all of them were just eating in peace.

EXPANDING YOUR PRACTICE

SILENT RETREATS AND GROUP MEDITATION

Silent retreats and group meditations are very powerful, primarily for two reasons: In a group setting, we are encouraged to commit to our meditation. Any excuses that would make us end our meditation earlier dissolve when we commit to meditating as a group for a specific time. Secondly, you get to connect with like-minded people who practice meditation. This is so valuable in our modern world, in which there is a lot of disconnection, and chances are that we don't have many friends who meditate. These connections can light up your life beyond just a meditation retreat or a group meditation.

Whether you are just starting with meditation or looking to expand your practice, doing a meditation retreat can help you deepen your practice and dedicate a certain number of days just to meditate. In our daily lives, we are so busy, and while every moment we spend in meditation is precious, there is a magic that comes with dedicating a few days in a row solely to meditation. Most meditation retreats also come with noble silence, which means there is no communication between participants, no phone or other technology. This means there is no distraction other than our own mind. When you are looking to do your first meditation retreat, there are some things to consider such as the style of meditation, the number of days, and the rules of the retreat. Trust your heart in whatever resonates with you.

Here are some possible options:

My teacher, davidji, offers 5-day *Sacred Soul* retreats in the US, in which silence is explored through meditation, heart-based yoga, and somatic practices. There are two days of silence during the retreat.

If you feel that discipline and structure could help you to expand your practice, you can consider a *Vipassana* retreat. These 10-day retreats originate from the Buddha's teachings and are offered free of charge, based on donations, all over the world. The retreat focused first on developing concentration by calming the mind, to then practice insight or *Vipassana*. There is a strict schedule, and silence is practiced for the entire ten days.

If you are looking for a more heart-based approach to meditation, you might resonate with a school called *Hridaya Yoga*. They offer 3-day, 10-day, and 17-day meditation retreats in Mexico and Europe. The practice is focused on deepening into Hridaya, the Spiritual Heart, and includes meditation, lectures, and hatha yoga. Silence is practiced for the entire duration of the retreat.

If all you are looking for right now is a group meditation, you can start on the Insight Timer app, as there are live meditation classes offered. For in-person classes in your area, you can look for offers in your local Buddhist community, at universities, or community centers. If you can't find a suitable group meditation, why not start your own? Just meditating together with a group in silence can have profound effects on our practice. It is very beautiful to practice Metta together as a group at the end of the session to send blessings to the world.

EXPLORING DIFFERENT MEDITATION STYLES

Throughout this book, we have explored different styles of meditation. Ultimately, the aim of meditation, no matter the style, is to deepen into the true essence of our Being. Different meditation styles show different ways to the same outcome. It is up to us to find a branch of meditation that resonates with us – as many meditation practitioners, as many paths! If you like to keep it simple, you can continue practicing mindfulness meditation by focusing your attention on an object. Perhaps you are a person who enjoys working with energies – in this case, you might want to include chakra meditation into your daily practice. If you like the idea of practicing meditation with a mantra, you might enjoy transcendental meditation. In this meditation style, you keep repeating a phrase or mantra until you feel a state of inner well-being and calmness.[5] The mind is focused on the mantra until you transcend into deeper states of consciousness. If you are looking for a meditation style that focuses on the heart, you might resonate with *Hridaya Yoga*. This style of meditation uses the heart center as an anchor and helps practitioners to find a way back to their Essence deep within in the heart. Alternatively, if you enjoy heart-based meditation, you can also incorporate gratitude and Metta you're your daily practice. If you are looking for a clear, structured path based on discipline, you can consider various styles of Buddhist meditation, such as Vipassana or Zen. For example, in Zen Buddhism, zazen is practiced as a form of sitting meditation in which a strong posture is assumed, and practitioners focus on the breath as the object of meditation. The idea in Zen Buddhism is that stillness is found in the present moment. Nothing is to be done, other than deepening into the present moment.[6] In Vipassana, the additional step of insight is added. If you enjoy working with the body, you can explore hatha yoga as meditation in movement. These are just some examples of meditation styles – there are many more to explore!

PERSONAL GROWTH THROUGH ADVANCED MEDITATION PRACTICES

At the beginning of our meditation path, we often stick to just one meditation style that we are comfortable with. For one of my students, Anna, this was mindfulness meditation. She started using her breath as an object and then over time alternated with a flower, candle flame, and picture of a deity. She enjoyed her meditations and saw many aspects of her life transforming over the years. Then, at some point, she ended up doing a *Vipassana* retreat. She told me how life-changing it was, as for most of her meditation journey, she thought focusing on an object is all there is to meditation. Adding the next step of *Insight* made her access deeper states of consciousness very quickly; her mind was trained in concentration for years and thus ready for deeper meditation. After the Vipassana retreat, Anna quit her corporate job, moved across the country, and became a meditation teacher as she had a direct insight into her true Essence. She found her true Soul's path. It was by opening to these advanced meditation techniques that this shift was possible.

THE ONGOING JOURNEY

REFLECTION AND GOAL SETTING

Especially in the beginning, it is a great idea to have a meditation diary. You can commit to journaling about your meditation journey for the first month, or longer if you feel like it. If you like to follow a structured process for reflection, you can write down the length of your meditation every day, the general qualities of the meditation (for example, "distracted", or "clear"), how you felt after the meditation, and the general quality of your entire day. At the end of the period, you can read through your diary and reflect on the connection between your meditation practice and your daily life. If you prefer an unstructured reflection, you can take a moment after your meditation to journal on whatever your heart wants to express.

Additionally, as you start your practice, it can be powerful to have a "check-in" with yourself at the end of each week, to see how you feel about your meditation practice, and whether it's time to try a different style or to add another form of meditation.

If you are a person who enjoys setting goals for everything, including your meditation practice, it can be helpful to focus on how you want to feel as a result of the meditation practice, or what situations in your life you would like to transform. For example, you could set a goal that you would like to feel more grateful for in life or that you would like to feel less distracted at

121

work. This generally works better than setting unrealistic goals regarding the duration of the practice. To have a goal of meditating daily for 2 hours in your first month of meditating might put a lot of pressure on you, whereas you want to enjoy meditation. It is advised to start slowly, for example, with meditating 5 or 10 minutes a day, and to then add a few minutes every week. As always, use your own discernment and internal guidance system.

STAYING COMMITTED TO GROWTH

At some point, you might find that there are days on which you really don't feel like meditating. Often, we start with a lot of enthusiasm and commitment and find ourselves less motivated to keep up our consistent practice. In these times, it's important to remember our intention for starting a meditation practice and to reflect on how our life has changed as a result of meditation. In the end, all of us long to become our most authentic versions and to live our fullest potential. This is the path of meditation. If you feel like you can't get back to your initial enthusiasm, you can look for a group meditation, add new styles of meditation, or set a new goal. Also, we have to remember that how we do anything is how we do everything. The way we show up for our meditation reflects how we show up in all areas of life. Therefore, whenever you feel like you are in a "meditation low", it is wise to reflect on the general quality of your life. Can you see a connection between meditation and the rest of your life? Can staying committed to your meditation practice help you to stay committed to your evolution and growth in all aspects of life?

THE CONTINUOUS EVOLUTION OF A DEDICATED MEDITATOR

Perhaps you can recall the metaphor we used earlier in the book – a meditation student ascending the mountain with the elephant and monkey. On the continuous journey of meditation, we can refer to this story to understand where we are at and what can help us to evolve further on our journey. It also shows us that we evolve on our meditation path, even if it's not obvious to us. On this journey up the mountain, it is normal to encounter roadblocks, to lose sight during foggy days, to fall and get back up, and to rest and enjoy the view. The key to all of this is to remain loving and compassionate with us. With self-compassion, any obstacle and setback can be turned into opportunity and growth. And after all, if the path of meditation was easy and completed within one week – what's the point? Isn't it exactly this journey of evolution, constant growth, and deepening into the true Essence of ourselves that makes meditation so special? Of learning to love ourselves through all of this?

CONCLUSION

As we reach the conclusion of this journey through the inner realms of peace and self-discovery, it's essential to acknowledge the profound transformation that meditation can bring to our lives. The seeds of meditation were planted in my teenage years and have made a profound difference in my life. My hope for you now that we've explored the depths of mindfulness, delved into the power of breath, and embraced the beauty of stillness is that meditation can have a profound effect on your life, too. We've learned that meditation is not merely a practice but a way of life—a path that leads us back to ourselves, time and time again.

In the quiet moments of reflection, may you remember that you are not alone on this journey. Countless souls around the world are walking this path alongside you (275 million), seeking the same peace and understanding. Let's continue to support and uplift one another as we navigate the complexities of existence with grace and compassion. With each step we take (and with each breath we take), may we illuminate the world with the radiant light of mindfulness and love. Thank you for allowing me to be a part of your journey. And thank you to every hard knock, life lesson, invited and uninvited teacher, and loving embrace that showed me the way to a better version of myself. I'll leave you with one last mantra: Ananda Maya Moksha. Ananda is bliss and/or happiness. Maya is the illusion of sadness and/or depression. Moksha is the freedom and/or liberation. Ananda Maya Moksha – free ourselves from life's negative illusions.

Namaste, Beautiful Soul.

BONUS MATERIALS

Take a moment to share some meditations with me. Scan the QR codes and join me in meditation.

Metta – Unconditional Loving Kindness Meditation
In this variation of a Metta meditation, we are sending out unconditional loving kindness into the world as we breath in and release all of that delicious energy to every corner of the globe and cosmos!

Tonglen Meditation
In this meditation, we will breathe, relax, settle in and change the world by changing ourselves.

Subscribe to my YouTube Channel
Find more meditations and insights.

Golden Alchemy Meditation Website

Sign up for FREE Meditations
Meditations are delivered to your inbox monthly, along with exclusive offers and education.

REFERENCES

CHAPTER ONE

[1] Theimer, S. (2023, October 26). Your body knows the difference between good stress and bad stress: Do you? Mayo Clinic News Network. https://newsnetwork.mayoclinic.org/discussion/your-body-knows-the-difference-between-good-stress-and-bad-stress-do-you/

[2] Summa Health. (2021, January 18). Stress Management: How to Tell the Difference Between Good and Bad Stress. Summa Health Flourish. https://www.summahealth.org/flourish/entries/2021/01/stress-management-how-to-tell-the-difference-between-good-and-bad-stress#:~:text=Good%20stress%2C%20or%20eustress%2C%20is,go%20on%20a%20first%20date

[3] Medline Plus. (n.d.). Stress. Medline Plus. https://medlineplus.gov/stress.html

[4] Scott, E. (2023, October 1). What is acute stress? Learn about this common occurrence. Verywellmind. https://www.verywellmind.com/all-about-acute-stress-3145064

[5] Harvard Health Publishing. (2020, July 6). Staying Healthy - Understanding the stress response. Harvard Medical School. https://www.health.harvard.edu/staying-healthy/understanding-the-stress-response

[6] Mastroianni, B. (2020, May 17). Why Americans are more stressed today than they were in the 1990s. Healthline. https://www.healthline.com/health-news/people-more-stressed-today-than-1990s

[7] University Hospitals. (2015, July 2). The top 5 most stressful life events and how to handle them. The science of health. https://www.uhhospitals.org/blog/articles/2015/07/the-top-5-most-stressful-life-events

[8] CAHMH. (n.d.). Stress. https://www.camh.ca/en/health-info/mental-illness-and-addiction-index/stress

[9] Britannica. (n.d.). Vedic religion. https://www.britannica.com/topic/Vedic-religion

[10] Khan Academy. (n.d.). The history of Buddhism. https://www.khanacademy.org/humanities/world-history/ancient-medieval/early-indian-empires/a/buddhism-in-indian-culture

[11] Chow, S. (n.d.). Meditation history. News medical life sciences. https://www.news-medical.net/health/Meditation-History.aspx

[12] Cleveland Clinic. (n.d.). Meditation. https://my.clevelandclinic.org/health/articles/17906-meditation

[13] Science Daily. (2011, January 21). Mindfulness meditation training changes brain structure in eight weeks. Science News. https://www.sciencedaily.com/releases/2011/01/110121144007.htm

[14] Desai, K., Gupta, P., Parikh, P., & Desai, A. (Year). Impact of Virtual Heartfulness Meditation Program on Stress, Quality of Sleep, and Psychological Wellbeing during the COVID-19 Pandemic: A Mixed-Method Study. Int. J. Environ. Res. PublicHealth, Volume, Page numbers. https://www.mdpi.com/1660-4601/18/21/11114/pdf

[15] Beach, S. R. (n.d.). Create a Meditation Space in your home. Left brain buddha. https://leftbrainbuddha.com/create-a-meditation-space-in-your-home/

CHAPTER TWO

[1] Insight Timer. (n.d.). Drishti meaning in yoga. Retrieved from
https://insighttimer.com/blog/drishti-meaning-yoga/

[2] Escoffier, N. (n.d.). The Seven Point Posture of Vairocana. Retrieved from
https://nicolasescoffier.com/seven-point-posture-vairocana/

[3] Fincham, G. W., Strauss, C., Montero-Marin, J., & Cavanagh, K. (2023, January 9). Effect of breathwork on stress and mental health: A meta-analysis of randomised-controlled trials. *Scientific Reports, 13,* Retrieved from:
https://www.nature.com/articles/s41598-022-27247-y

[4] Zaccaro, A., Piarulli, A., Laurino, M., Garbella, E., Menicucci, D., Neri, B., & Gemignani, A. (2018). How Breath-Control Can Change Your Life: A Systematic Review on Psycho-Physiological Correlates of Slow Breathing. *Frontiers in Human Neuroscience, 12,* Article 353.
https://doi.org/10.3389/fnhum.2018.00353

[5] Calm. (n.d.). Box Breathing. Retrieved from
https://www.calm.com/blog/box-breathing

[6] Mindful. (n.d.). What is mindfulness? Retrieved from
https://www.mindful.org/what-is-mindfulness/

[7] Sadhguru. (n.d.). Cultivating Awareness. Retrieved from
https://isha.sadhguru.org/en/wisdom/article/cultivating-awareness

[8] Insight Timer. (n.d.). Home page. Retrieved from
https://insighttimer.com

[9] Headspace. (n.d.). Home page. Retrieved from
https://www.headspace.com

[10] Calm. (n.d.). Home page. Retrieved from
https://www.calm.com

[11] Davidj. (n.d.). About Davidji. Retrieved from
https://davidji.com/about/

[12] Mindworks. (n.d.). What is guided meditation? Retrieved from https://mindworks.org/blog/what-is-guided-meditation/

[13] Yoga Basics. (n.d.). Visualization Meditation. Retrieved from https://www.yogabasics.com/connect/yoga-blog/visualization-meditation/

[14] Puff, R. (2021, February 8). The Journey Toward Inner Peace. *Psychology Today*. Retrieved from: https://www.psychologytoday.com/us/blog/meditation-modern-life/202102/the-journey-toward-inner-peace

[15] Puff, R. (2021, February 8). The Journey Toward Inner Peace. *Psychology Today*. Retrieved from: https://www.psychologytoday.com/us/blog/meditation-modern-life/202102/the-journey-toward-inner-peace

[16] HelpGuide. (n.d.). Body Scan Meditation. Retrieved from https://www.helpguide.org/meditations/body-scan-meditation.htm

CHAPTER THREE

[1] Stress.org. (n.d.). 42 Worrying Workplace Stress Statistics. https://www.stress.org/42-worrying-workplace-stress-statistics

[2] Calm. (n.d.). Box Breathing. https://www.calm.com/blog/box-breathing

[3] Sri Sri School of Yoga. (n.d.). Nadi Shodhana: Learn All About Alternate Nostril Breathing. https://srisrischoolofyoga.org/na/blog/nadi-shodhana-learn-all-about-alternate-nostril-breathing/

[4] Saumya Ayurveda. (n.d.). Nadi Shodhana Alternate Nostril Breathing Guide. https://www.saumya-ayurveda.com/post/nadi-shodhana-alternate-nostril-breathing-guide

[5] Sri Sri School of Yoga. (n.d.). Nadi Shodhana: Learn All About Alternate Nostril Breathing. https://srisrischoolofyoga.org/na/blog/nadi-shodhana-learn-all-about-alternate-nostril-breathing/

[6] Headspace. (n.d.). Body Scan. https://www.headspace.com/meditation/body-scan

[7] Headspace. (n.d.). Body Scan. https://www.headspace.com/meditation/body-scan

[8] Verywell Mind. (n.d.). Body Scan Meditation: Why and How. https://www.verywellmind.com/body-scan-meditation-why-and-how-3144782

[9] Anxiety Canada. (n.d.). How to Do Progressive Muscle Relaxation. https://www.anxietycanada.com/articles/how-to-do-progressive-muscle-relaxation/

[10] Anxiety Canada. (n.d.). How to Do Progressive Muscle Relaxation. https://www.anxietycanada.com/articles/how-to-do-progressive-muscle-relaxation/

[11] Greater Good Science Center. (n.d.). Definition of Compassion. https://greatergood.berkeley.edu/topic/compassion/definition

[12] Hridaya Yoga Teacher Training, Month 1 Booklet.

[13] The Guardian. (2014, August 27). Murder trial of Tibetan Lama begins. https://www.theguardian.com/world/2014/aug/27/murder-trial-akong-rinpoche-tibetan-lama-begins

[14] Chopra. (n.d.). 8 Ways to Practice Compassion for a Healthier and Stronger Relationship. https://chopra.com/blogs/personal-growth/8-ways-to-practice-compassion-for-a-healthier-and-stronger-relationship

[15] American Psychological Association. (2013, April). Marriage: The biggest cause of stress?

https://www.apa.org/monitor/2013/04/marriage

[16] Chopra. (n.d.). 8 Ways to Practice Compassion for a Healthier and Stronger Relationship.
https://chopra.com/blogs/personal-growth/8-ways-to-practice-compassion-for-a-healthier-and-stronger-relationship

[17] Now Here Global. (n.d.). Compassionate Communication.
https://www.now-here.global/compassionate-communication

[18] Now Here Global. (n.d.). Compassionate Communication.
https://www.now-here.global/compassionate-communication

[19] Now Here Global. (n.d.). Compassionate Communication.
https://www.now-here.global/compassionate-communication

[20] Metta Institute. (n.d.). Metta Meditation.
https://www.mettainstitute.org/mettameditation.html

[21] Metta Institute. (n.d.). Metta Meditation.
https://www.mettainstitute.org/mettameditation.html

CHAPTER FOUR

[1] Emotion Researcher. (2015, March). The Component Process Model of Emotion, and the Power of Coincidences | Emotion Researcher. Retrieved from
http://emotionresearcher.com/the-component-process-model-of-emotion-and-the-power-of-coincidences/

[2] PositivePsychology.com. (n.d.). Emotion Wheel. Retrieved from
https://positivepsychology.com/emotion-wheel/

[3] PositivePsychology.com. (n.d.). Emotion Wheel. Retrieved from
https://positivepsychology.com/emotion-wheel/

[4] PositivePsychology.com. (n.d.). Emotion Wheel. Retrieved from
https://positivepsychology.com/emotion-wheel/

[5] PositivePsychology.com. (n.d.). Emotion Wheel. Retrieved from https://positivepsychology.com/emotion-wheel/

[6] PositivePsychology.com. (n.d.). Emotion Wheel. Retrieved from https://positivepsychology.com/emotion-wheel/

[7] Psych Central. (n.d.). Emotion Wheel. Retrieved from https://psychcentral.com/health/emotion-wheel#what-is-it

[8] Psych Central. (n.d.). Emotion Wheel. Retrieved from https://psychcentral.com/health/emotion-wheel#what-is-it

[9] Woodall-Carroll, D. (n.d.). The Relationship Between Thoughts, Feelings, and Behaviors. Retrieved from https://debbiewoodallcarroll.com/the-relationship-between-thoughts-feelings-and-behaviors/

[10] Hawkins, D. R. (2013). *Letting Go: The Pathway of Surrender* (1st Hay House edition). Hay House, Inc.

[11] Hawkins, D. R. (2013). *Letting Go: The Pathway of Surrender* (1st Hay House edition). Hay House, Inc.

[12] LaViolette, P. A. (1979). Thoughts about Thoughts about Thoughts: The Emotional-Perceptive Cycle Theory. Man-Environment Systems, 9(1), 15-47.

[13] Van der Kolk, B. A. (2014). The Body Keeps the Score.

[14] Ananda. (n.d.). Meditation for Balance & Equilibrium. Retrieved from https://www.ananda.org/video/meditation-for-balance-equilibrium/

[15] Hawkins, D. R. (2013). *Letting Go: The Pathway of Surrender* (1st Hay House edition). Hay House, Inc.

[16] Sedona Training Associates. (n.d.). Suppress and Express. Retrieved from https://www.sedona.com/Suppress-and-Express.asp

[17] Hawkins, D. R. (2013). *Letting Go: The Pathway of Surrender* (1st Hay House edition). Hay House, Inc.

[18] Hawkins, D. R. (2013). *Letting Go: The Pathway of Surrender* (1st Hay House edition). Hay House, Inc.

[19] Choosing Therapy. (n.d.). Meditation for Anger. Retrieved from https://www.choosingtherapy.com/meditation-for-anger/

[20] Choosing Therapy. (n.d.). Meditation for Anger. Retrieved from https://www.choosingtherapy.com/meditation-for-anger/

[21] Harvard Health Publishing. (2014, January 8). Mindfulness Meditation May Ease Anxiety, Mental Stress. Retrieved from https://www.health.harvard.edu/blog/mindfulness-meditation-may-ease-anxiety-mental-stress-201401086967

[22] Harvard Health Publishing. (2014, January 8). Mindfulness Meditation May Ease Anxiety, Mental Stress. Retrieved from https://www.health.harvard.edu/blog/mindfulness-meditation-may-ease-anxiety-mental-stress-201401086967

[23] Calm. (n.d.). How to Meditate for Anxiety. Retrieved from https://www.calm.com/blog/how-to-meditate-for-anxiety

[24] PositivePsychology.com. (n.d.). Gratitude & Appreciation. Retrieved from https://positivepsychology.com/gratitude-appreciation/

[25] Greater Good Science Center. (n.d.). How Gratitude Changes You and Your Brain. Retrieved from https://greatergood.berkeley.edu/article/item/how_gratitude_changes_yo u_and_your_brain?fbclid=lwAR1N-g-VhfKpeAWa17SW-Nl9Ey5lv6BOAnzyuavntBOGUYpn2p2dl-_UVd0

[26] Mindful Anger. (2022, March). Why Forgive? Because It's Good for You. Retrieved from https://www.psychologytoday.com/us/blog/mindful-anger/202203/why-forgive-because-it-s-good-you

[27] PositivePsychology.com. (n.d.). How to Practice Self-Compassion. Retrieved from https://positivepsychology.com/how-to-practice-self-compassion/

[28] PositivePsychology.com. (n.d.). How to Practice Self-Compassion. Retrieved from https://positivepsychology.com/how-to-practice-self-compassion/

[29] Mindful Anger. (2022, March). Why Forgive? Because It's Good for You. Retrieved from https://www.psychologytoday.com/us/blog/mindful-anger/202203/why-forgive-because-it-s-good-you

CHAPTER FIVE

[1] Dickson, J. (n.d.). Evolving Attention Span: Rethinking Education in the Digital Age. Retrieved from https://www.linkedin.com/pulse/evolving-attention-span-rethinking-education-digital-age-dickson

[2] Hutton, J. T., & Colleagues. (2018). The effects of digital technology on attention span and academic performance: Implications for education. Journal of Educational Technology, 37(4), 512-526. Retrieved from https://www.ncbi.nlm.nih.gov/pmc/articles/PMC6088366/

[3] BetterUp. (n.d.). 15 Ways to Improve Your Focus and Concentration Skills. Retrieved from https://www.betterup.com/blog/15-ways-to-improve-your-focus-and-concentration-skills

[4] BetterUp. (n.d.). 15 Ways to Improve Your Focus and Concentration Skills. Retrieved from https://www.betterup.com/blog/15-ways-to-improve-your-focus-and-concentration-skills

[5] Little Flower Yoga. (n.d.). Single Pointed Focus Meditation. Retrieved from

https://www.littlefloweryoga.com/blog/single-pointed-focus-meditation/

[6] Fassbender, E. (2015). Mindfulness meditation for enhancing attention regulation in university students. Frontiers in Psychology, 6, 1532. Retrieved from
https://www.ncbi.nlm.nih.gov/pmc/articles/PMC4449168/

[7] Headspace. (n.d.). Meditation for Productivity. Retrieved from
https://www.headspace.com/meditation/productivity

[8] Fassbender, E. (2015). Mindfulness meditation for enhancing attention regulation in university students. Frontiers in Psychology, 6, 1532. Retrieved from
https://www.ncbi.nlm.nih.gov/pmc/articles/PMC4449168/

[9] Mindful. (n.d.). 10 Ways to Be More Mindful at Work. Retrieved from
https://www.mindful.org/10-ways-mindful-work/

[10] Mindful. (n.d.). 10 Ways to Be More Mindful at Work. Retrieved from
https://www.mindful.org/10-ways-mindful-work/

[11] Shrestha, A., & Colleagues. (2022). Impact of digital distractions on work performance: A systematic review. Journal of Digital Behavior, 3(1), 45-62. Retrieved from
https://www.ncbi.nlm.nih.gov/pmc/articles/PMC8598050/

[12] Piedmont Healthcare. (n.d.). Does Your Smartphone Cause Anxiety? Retrieved from
https://www.piedmont.org/living-real-change/does-your-smartphone-cause-anxiety

[13] Piedmont Healthcare. (n.d.). Does Your Smartphone Cause Anxiety? Retrieved from
https://www.piedmont.org/living-real-change/does-your-smartphone-cause-anxiety

[14] DIY Genius. (n.d.). Digital Mindfulness: Finding Balance in the Digital Age. Retrieved from
https://www.diygenius.com/digital-mindfulness/

CHAPTER SIX

[1] Terebess. (n.d.). The Ten Oxherding Pictures: 27. Retrieved from https://terebess.hu/english/oxherd27.html

[2] Age of Awareness. (n.d.). Four Stages of Meditation Anyone Who Meditates Should Know. Retrieved from https://medium.com/age-of-awareness/four-stages-of-meditation-anyone-who-meditates-should-know-b7f42ed71641

[3] Age of Awareness. (n.d.). Four Stages of Meditation Anyone Who Meditates Should Know. Retrieved from https://medium.com/age-of-awareness/four-stages-of-meditation-anyone-who-meditates-should-know-b7f42ed71641

[4] Age of Awareness. (n.d.). Four Stages of Meditation Anyone Who Meditates Should Know. Retrieved from https://medium.com/age-of-awareness/four-stages-of-meditation-anyone-who-meditates-should-know-b7f42ed71641

[5] Ignite Yoga Dayton. (n.d.). What is the Gap in Meditation? Retrieved from https://igniteyogadayton.com/what-is-the-gap-in-meditation/

[6] Path of Sincerity. (n.d.). Insight Meditation (aka Vipassana): The What, Why & How. Retrieved from https://www.pathofsincerity.com/insight-meditation-aka-vipassana-the-what-why-how/

[7] Path of Sincerity. (n.d.). Insight Meditation (aka Vipassana): The What, Why & How. Retrieved from https://www.pathofsincerity.com/insight-meditation-aka-vipassana-the-what-why-how/

[8] Mindworks. (n.d.). Chakra Meditation: A Guide to This Ancient Practice. Retrieved from https://mindworks.org/blog/chakra-meditation/

[9] Arhanta Yoga. (n.d.). 7 Chakras: An Introduction to the Energy Centers & Their Effect. Retrieved from
https://www.arhantayoga.org/blog/7-chakras-introduction-energy-centers-effect/

[10] Deconstructing Yourself. (n.d.). Mindfulness Reboot. Retrieved from
https://deconstructingyourself.com/mindfulness-reboot.html

[11] Deconstructing Yourself. (n.d.). Mindfulness Reboot. Retrieved from
https://deconstructingyourself.com/mindfulness-reboot.html

[12] Deconstructing Yourself. (n.d.). Mindfulness Reboot. Retrieved from
https://deconstructingyourself.com/mindfulness-reboot.html

[13] Australian School of Meditation & Yoga. (n.d.). A Meditation Ritual That Will Transform Your Life. Retrieved from
https://asmy.org.au/meditation/a-meditation-ritual-that-will-transform-your-life/

[14] Search Inside Yourself Leadership Institute. (n.d.). Consistent Meditation Practice. Retrieved from
https://siyli.org/consistent-meditation-practice/

CHAPTER SEVEN

[1] National Center for Biotechnology Information. (n.d.). Sleep Deprivation and Deficiency. Retrieved from
https://www.ncbi.nlm.nih.gov/pmc/articles/PMC6473877/

[2] Somnology MD. (2018). Facts About Sleep Deprivation. Retrieved from
https://www.somnologymd.com/2018/01/facts-about-sleep-deprivation/

[3] National Center for Biotechnology Information. (n.d.). Sleep Deprivation and Deficiency. Retrieved from
https://www.ncbi.nlm.nih.gov/pmc/articles/PMC6473877/

[4] Pharma News Intel. (2023). CDC Analyzes Sleep Medication Usage by Adults in the United States. Retrieved from

https://pharmanewsintel.com/news/cdc-analyzes-sleep-medication-usage-by-adults-in-the-united-states#:~:text=February%2015%2C%202023%20%2D%20A%20recent,sleep%20medication%20across%20the%20US

[5] Oregon Health & Science University. (n.d.). Understanding Sleep Disorders. Retrieved from https://www.ohsu.edu/brain-institute/understanding-sleep-disorders

[6] Cleveland Clinic. (n.d.). Sleep Disorders. Retrieved from https://my.clevelandclinic.org/health/diseases/11429-sleep-disorder

[7] Oregon Health & Science University. (n.d.). Understanding Sleep Disorders. Retrieved from https://www.ohsu.edu/brain-institute/understanding-sleep-disorders

[8] Cleveland Clinic. (n.d.). Sleep Disorders. Retrieved from https://my.clevelandclinic.org/health/diseases/11429-sleep-disorders

[9] Oregon Health & Science University. (n.d.). Understanding Sleep Disorders. Retrieved from https://www.ohsu.edu/brain-institute/understanding-sleep-disorders

[10] Cleveland Clinic. (n.d.). Sleep Disorders. Retrieved from https://my.clevelandclinic.org/health/diseases/11429-sleep-disorders

[11] Cleveland Clinic. (n.d.). Sleep Disorders. Retrieved from https://my.clevelandclinic.org/health/diseases/11429-sleep-disorders

[12] Ong, J. C., Manber, R., Segal, Z., Xia, Y., Shapiro, S., & Wyatt, J. K. (2014). A randomized controlled trial of mindfulness meditation for chronic insomnia. Sleep, 37(9), 1553-1563.

[13] Thimmapuram, J., Yommer, D., Tudor, L., Bell, T., Dumitrescu, C., & Davis, R. (2020). Heartfulness meditation improves sleep in chronic insomnia. Journal of Community Hospital Internal Medicine Perspectives, 10(1), 10-15.

[14] Ong, J. C., Manber, R., Segal, Z., Xia, Y., Shapiro, S., & Wyatt, J. K. (2014). A randomized controlled trial of mindfulness meditation for chronic insomnia. Sleep, 37(9), 1553-1563.

[15] National Sleep Foundation. (n.d.). Meditation for Sleep. Retrieved from
https://www.sleepfoundation.org/meditation-for-sleep

[16] One Yoga Thailand. (n.d.). Yoga Nidra: Step-by-Step Guide to Yogic Sleep for Top Relaxation. Retrieved from
https://oneyogathailand.com/yoga-nidra-step-by-step-guide-to-yogic-sleep-for-top-relaxation/

[17] National Sleep Foundation. (n.d.). How to Fall Asleep Fast. Retrieved from
https://www.sleepfoundation.org/sleep-hygiene/how-to-fall-asleep-fast

[18] National Center for Biotechnology Information. (n.d.). Mindfulness-Based Therapy for Insomnia. Retrieved from
https://www.ncbi.nlm.nih.gov/pmc/articles/PMC9623891/

[19] Chopra. (n.d.). 9 Powerful Mantras in Sanskrit and Gurmukhi. Retrieved from
https://chopra.com/blogs/personal-growth/9-powerful-mantras-in-sanskrit-and-gurmukhi

[20] Eugene Therapy. (n.d.). Create a Mindful Morning Routine. Retrieved from
https://eugenetherapy.com/article/create-a-mindful-morning-routine/

CHAPTER EIGHT

[1] Mindworks. (n.d.). Self-Reflection Meditation: A Guide to Inner Awareness. Retrieved from
https://mindworks.org/blog/self-reflection-meditation

[2] Verywell Mind. (n.d.). Self-Reflection: Importance, Benefits, and Strategies. Retrieved from https://www.verywellmind.com/self-reflection-importance-benefits-and-strategies-7500858

[3] Behavior Design. (n.d.). Using Meditation to Reprogram Your Mind. Retrieved from https://medium.com/behavior-design/using-meditation-to-reprogram-your-mind-7206b02ba807

[4] Chopra. (n.d.). 6 Ways Meditation Can Transcend Limiting Beliefs. Retrieved from https://chopra.com/blogs/meditation/6-ways-meditation-can-transcend-limiting-beliefs

[5] Chopra. (n.d.). 6 Ways Meditation Can Transcend Limiting Beliefs. Retrieved from https://chopra.com/blogs/meditation/6-ways-meditation-can-transcend-limiting-beliefs

[6] Behavior Design. (n.d.). Using Meditation to Reprogram Your Mind. Retrieved from https://medium.com/behavior-design/using-meditation-to-reprogram-your-mind-7206b02ba807

[7] Chopra. (n.d.). 6 Ways Meditation Can Transcend Limiting Beliefs. Retrieved from https://chopra.com/blogs/meditation/6-ways-meditation-can-transcend-limiting-beliefs

[8] Observer. (2017). Paying Attention to Details in Life: The Power of Mindfulness. Retrieved from https://observer.com/2017/03/mindfulness-pay-attention-details-life/

[9] Hridaya Yoga. (n.d.). Samskaras and Vasanas: Understanding Subconscious Tendencies. Retrieved from https://hridaya-yoga.com/samskaras-and-vasanas-subconscious-tendencies/

[10] Verywell Mind. (n.d.). Understanding Mindfulness-Based Relationship Enhancement (MBRE). Retrieved from https://www.verywellmind.com/understanding-mindfulness-based-relationship-enhancement-4685242

[11] Verywell Mind. (n.d.). Understanding Mindfulness-Based Relationship Enhancement (MBRE). Retrieved from https://www.verywellmind.com/understanding-mindfulness-based-relationship-enhancement-4685242

[12] Verywell Mind. (n.d.). Understanding Mindfulness-Based Relationship Enhancement (MBRE). Retrieved from https://www.verywellmind.com/understanding-mindfulness-based-relationship-enhancement-4685242

[13] Operation Meditation. (n.d.). Letting Go of the Past in 7 Simple Steps. Retrieved from https://operationmeditation.com/discover/letting-go-of-the-past-in-7-simple-steps/

[14] Mind Body Green. (n.d.). How to Set Intentions: A Guide to Manifesting Your Desires. Retrieved from https://www.mindbodygreen.com/articles/how-to-set-intentions

[15] Mind Body Green. (n.d.). How to Set Intentions: A Guide to Manifesting Your Desires. Retrieved from https://www.mindbodygreen.com/articles/how-to-set-intentions

CHAPTER NINE

[1] Seattle Anxiety. (2022, October 25). Mindfulness: Armor Against Anxiety. Retrieved from https://seattleanxiety.com/psychiatrist/2022/10/25/mindfulness-armor-against-anxiety

[2] Greater Good Magazine. (n.d.). Five Science-Backed Strategies to Build Resilience. Retrieved from

https://greatergood.berkeley.edu/article/item/five_science_backed_strateg ies_to_build_resilience

[3] Mind. (n.d.). Managing Stress and Building Resilience. Retrieved from https://www.mind.org.uk/information-support/types-of-mental-health-problems/stress/managing-stress-and-building-resilience/

[4] Psych Central. (n.d.). 10 Tips to Build Resilience. Retrieved from https://psychcentral.com/lib/10-tips-to-build-resilience#4

[5] Johns Hopkins Medicine. (n.d.). Gangrene Overview. Retrieved from https://www.hopkinsmedicine.org/health/conditions-and-diseases/gangrene#:~:text=What%20is%20gangrene%3F,skin%20a%20gre enish%2Dblack%20color

[6] Mindworks. (n.d.). Meditation for Healing: A Guide to Inner Well-being. Retrieved from https://mindworks.org/blog/meditation-for-healing/

[7] Encyclopædia Britannica. (n.d.). Psychosomatic Disorder. Retrieved from https://www.britannica.com/science/psychosomatic-disorder

[8] Better Health Channel. (n.d.). Placebo Effect. Retrieved from https://www.betterhealth.vic.gov.au/health/conditionsandtreatments/plac ebo-effect

[9] Dr. Joe Dispenza. (n.d.). Scientific Research. Retrieved from https://drjoedispenza.com/scientific-research

[10] Better Sleep Council. (n.d.). Meditation in Times of Grief: A Path to Peaceful Sleep. Retrieved from https://www.bettersleep.com/blog/meditation-in-times-of-grief/

[11] Better Sleep Council. (n.d.). Meditation in Times of Grief: A Path to Peaceful Sleep. Retrieved from https://www.bettersleep.com/blog/meditation-in-times-of-grief/

[12] Better Sleep Council. (n.d.). Meditation in Times of Grief: A Path to Peaceful Sleep. Retrieved from

https://www.bettersleep.com/blog/meditation-in-times-of-grief/

[13] Better Sleep Council. (n.d.). Meditation in Times of Grief: A Path to Peaceful Sleep. Retrieved from
https://www.bettersleep.com/blog/meditation-in-times-of-grief/

[14] Better Sleep Council. (n.d.). Meditation in Times of Grief: A Path to Peaceful Sleep. Retrieved from
https://www.bettersleep.com/blog/meditation-in-times-of-grief/

[15] National Center for Biotechnology Information. (n.d.). Mindfulness-Based Interventions in Rheumatoid Arthritis. Retrieved from
https://www.ncbi.nlm.nih.gov/pmc/articles/PMC7287297/

[16] Center for Healthy Minds. (n.d.). Meditation Can Help During Crisis and Everyday Lives. Retrieved from
https://www.centerhealthyminds.org/join-the-movement/meditation-can-help-during-crisis-and-everyday-lives

[17] National Center for Biotechnology Information. (n.d.). Meditation Programs for Psychological Stress and Well-being. Retrieved from
https://www.ncbi.nlm.nih.gov/pmc/articles/PMC4513203/

[18] Awaken. (2019). How to Cultivate Inner Strength Through Meditation. Retrieved from
https://awaken.com/2019/05/how-to-cultivate-inner-strength-through-meditation/

CHAPTER TEN

[1] Mindfulness Box. (n.d.). How Many People Meditate in the World? Retrieved from
https://mindfulnessbox.com/how-many-people-meditate-in-the-world/

[2] Yoga Vidya School. (n.d.). Meditation Statistics: How Many People Meditate Worldwide? Retrieved from
https://www.yogavidyaschool.com/blog/meditation-statistics

[3 National Center for Complementary and Integrative Health. (n.d.). Meditation and Mindfulness: What You Need to Know. Retrieved from https://www.nccih.nih.gov/health/meditation-and-mindfulness-what-you-need-to-know

[4] OneLife. (2021, June). Mini Moments of Mindfulness. Retrieved from https://www.onelifenz.com/blog/2021/6/mini-moments-of-mindfulness

[5] Transcendental Meditation. (n.d.). Transcendental Meditation Technique. Retrieved from https://www.tm.org/en-us/

[6] Path of Sincerity. (n.d.). Zen vs. Vipassana/Insight Meditation in Buddhism. Retrieved from https://www.pathofsincerity.com/zen-vs-vipassanainsight-meditation-buddhism/

www.ingramcontent.com/pod-product-compliance
Lightning Source LLC
Chambersburg PA
CBHW070717130626
46553CB00005B/2028